CELEBRATE THE EARTH

Other Books by Laurie Cabot

Power of the Witch: The Earth, the Moon, and the Magical Path to Enlightenment (with Tom Cowan)

Love Magic: The Way to Love Through Rituals, Spells and the Magical Life (with Tom Cowan)

CELEBRATE THE EARTH

A Year of Holidays in the Pagan Tradition

Laurie Cabot

with

Jean Mills

A Delta Book
Published by
Dell Publishing
a division of
Bantam Doubleday Dell Publishing Group, Inc.
1540 Broadway
New York, New York 10036

Grateful acknowledgment is made for permission to reprint the lyrics to the musical composition "Bring Back the Light" © 1987 e.v., Gypsy, appearing on pages 56–58.

Library of Congress Cataloging in Publication Data
Cabot, Laurie.
Celebrate the earth : a year of holidays in the Pagan tradition / by Laurie Cabot with Jean Mills.
p. cm.
Includes bibliographical references.
ISBN 0-385-30920-1
1. Fasts and feasts. 2. Witchcraft. 3. Religious calendars—Paganism. 4. Paganism. 5. Year—Religious aspects. I. Mills, Jean. II. Title.
BF 1572.F37C32 1994
299—dc20 94-4255 CIP

Manufactured in the United States of America
Published simultaneously in Canada

October 1994

10 9 8 7 6 5 4 3 2 1
BVG

For Edith Adrienne Van Cliff,

I thank you for your creative strength and sensitive nature, for inciting in me the power to stand like a Goddess, against all odds. Mother, I see your beauteous spirit in all seasons. The white silklike snow is the color of your skin; the blue crocus, the color of your eyes; the bright yellow Summer sun, the color of your voice, the Autumn rusts and reds, the auburn of your radiant hair. I love you always.

Your daughter,
Laurie

CONTENTS

Appendix:

Acknowledgments

I am deeply grateful to my grandson, Ari; my daughters, Jody and Penny Cabot and Alice Keegan for their patience, love, and support while I wrote this book; I am indebted to my treasured Witch family, Iain, Amy, and Richard, April Tuck, Lauren Dye, Jackie Phillips Bran, and Jeanie Crosby Chase, Sorine Patton, Anya Mitchell, Willette Brooks Wood, and Janice Giellford. I am thankful for my editor, Betsy Bundschuh, my agent, Susan Lee Cohen, the artistry of Karen Bagnard, and the support of my friends in the Witch community: Paula Forester, Lord Theodore Mills, Margie Fedele; I would like to acknowledge the work of Jean Renard, Otter and Morning Glory Zell, Diane Darling, Margot Adler, Janet and Stewart Farrar, Kerr Cuhulain, Ron Parshley, Karen Thorn, Tammy Medros; I would also like to acknowledge the memory of Scott Cunningham and Marie Willow Kelly; I am grateful to my Celtic ancestors for keeping the Faery magic alive, and . . . to all those "scholars" who failed to see that it is not just the mist and the sound of the sea in a quiet country that leads one to believe in magic. It is all of that and more, much more. It is science, art, and religion.

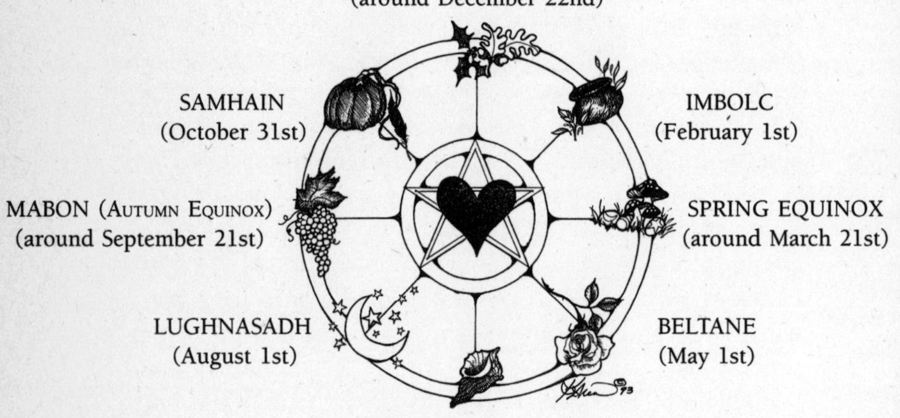
YULE (WINTER SOLSTICE)
(around December 22nd)
SAMHAIN
(October 31st)
IMBOLC
(February 1st)
MABON (AUTUMN EQUINOX)
(around September 21st)
SPRING EQUINOX
(around March 21st)
LUGHNASADH
(August 1st)
BELTANE
(May 1st)
MIDSUMMER (SUMMER SOLSTICE)
(around June 21st)

INTRODUCTION

As I have seen the world through Witch's eyes, I have been fortunate enough to live each moment of my life with the knowledge and deep feeling that the globe I walk upon feels *my* step, hears *my* voice, and answers in return. As a child I felt able to converse with the world about Her joy and pleasure. Upon my initiation as a Witch at the age of sixteen, I experienced an immediate intimacy with the Earth, Moon, and stars. This awakening became reality. Every dance I danced, every childlike chase, every handful of flowers, was a bonding of my heart and spirit with my Mother, the Earth.

In the vastness of our universe, seemingly unknowable and often hostile, our human voices sometimes seem small and insignificant. Our spirits cry out for something more, some connection which will prove that we matter, that we exist. In my own experience as a Witch, I can assure you that the universe and particularly our own planet, Mother Earth, *is* knowable to a great extent and not hostile to those willing to listen honestly to Her song.

The most extraordinary relationship that exists in creation is the bond between a mother and her children. We each sense this instinctively when we are born, but I recently had an experience that impressed upon me just how poignant and profound this relationship can be. I had no forewarning that evening about what was soon to take place, when a woman, a complete stranger, walked into my daughter's shop, where I receive my clients. She was an attractive, well-dressed woman, in her mid- to late forties, but she was visibly upset when I looked up into her eyes to greet her. She came to me seeking peace and answers to questions about her dead son. Her only child, her teenage son, had been killed in an auto accident about one month before. They had been very close, she said, at times more like friends than mother and son. She couldn't accept his death, that he was gone from her life. She felt bereft and lost.

She told me she knew nothing about the ways of Witchcraft, but that her son had taken an interest in magic and used to read lots of books on the subject. Not knowing which way to turn, she at last decided to come to me. She desperately wanted to know if her son was all right.

My heart went out to her: I was deeply moved by her story. My emotions were immediately engaged, and I wanted to comfort her. At the same time doubts arose within me about my ability to bring her some measure of peace, for I realized at once how distraught she was. I took a moment to reach inside myself for strength. I decided to approach her psychic reading just as I approach all my other counselings. I tried to put her at ease. She seemed to relax and I began to read her cards. Nothing could have prepared me for what happened next. I was well into my reading when I lifted my eyes from the tarot and saw the figure of a young man standing just over her left shoulder. I sensed that this was the essence of her beloved son.

So as not to disturb the rapport I had with the mother, I suppressed my own sudden feelings of surprise and wonder. I had not expected this. I quickly decided to prepare her for the message her son was attempting to send to her through me by explaining my beliefs, as a Witch, about death or the afterlife. Gently I told her that the choices for departed spirits are three. They can cross over into the Otherworld, a magical but very real place we call Summerland, where they can choose to stay forever. This is the land of milk and honey, peopled with our Gods and Goddesses and Faery Kings and Queens. The second choice is to be reincarnated and return to Earth in another capacity of service to the Great Goddess, our own Mother Earth. The third choice is to remain on the earthly plane as a ghost, until deciding either to cross over into Summerland or be reincarnated.

I told her that her son, for the time being, had comfortably chosen to be a ghost. Then I continued to say, as gently as I could so as not to frighten her, that he was standing right next to her at that very moment.

The woman was startled, then skeptical. As she tried to accept what I was saying, she quite naturally asked for some proof that he was truly there. She needed to know. She needed reassurance. I tried to give it to her by describing in detail what I saw and heard. I said, "He wants you to know that he is fine and not to worry about him, and he also wants you to know that this is his most prized possession."

With two hands, the boy proudly displayed before me a beautiful long sword that looked as if it were from the Civil War. The woman gasped. "We buried him with his great-great-grandfather's sword!"

Her son smiled, then told me to tell her that being a ghost felt a little like being the Highlander (a character in a movie of the same name). He said, "I feel like the Highlander, because I know I'm going to live forever."

Again the woman gasped. *The Highlander* was the last movie they saw together!

The young man asked me to reassure his mother that he was going to wait for her until the time came for her to cross over, and then together they would go to Summerland. "In the meantime," he said, "know that I am happy."

As a Witch or "walker between worlds," a term that is often used to describe Witches, I felt it a particular privilege to share in so vivid and meaningful an experience. The vision, and my revelations offered to the distraught mother, brought some semblance of peace to the woman and also served to reinforce my heartfelt conviction that there is nothing stronger than the love relationship between a mother and her children. I offer this story as a metaphor for the bond we each share with our Mother, the Earth. That bond is all-encompassing, always renewable, life sustaining, emotionally and physically satisfying, meeting all our needs, and answering all our questions. And yet it must be a reciprocal relationship in order for both Mother Earth and the human race to survive. With *Celebrate the Earth* I hope to demonstrate and offer to you the methods by which every human being can honor the Earth and play a part in the healing that must continue to take place.

I believe that the devastation of our planet in many cases is due not so much to negligence as to impersonality. We think of Earth as something apart from us, a separate entity, which exists on its own and will exist forever. It is my hope to awaken in you the notion that when one organism suffers, we all do. Each of us can make a direct contribution to Earth's well-being and come away with something deeply personal and of great importance, for the healing of Mother Earth is also a process of self-discovery.

When I became a Witch, I began to see people more as individuals and to realize how valuable it is to develop each individual's talents and gifts, whether it be the simple ability to communicate with others or the more complete ability to communicate psychically with other worlds. The mental projections and actions of every man, woman, and child on the planet combine to create the world in which we live. And yet many of us do not see or understand the magical power each of us wields. We are not aware of how strongly connected we are to the whole. We do not see ourselves as Her children and do not realize just how close to our Mother we are.

Each of us shares in a vital and timeless partnership with our planet. When we are young, we hold an intimate fascination for the world around us. But as we grow older, we get caught up in the hectic pace of a busy world. Time, in our society, weighs heavily upon our heads, but instead of being reckoned by the rising and setting of suns and moons, it is ticked off by the invasive blare of a clock radio or the high-pitched electronic tone of a digital watch. It is sad for me to think that for some of us, our feet never really touch the ground. These are people who are compelled for whatever reason to walk from house to paved driveway to car to concrete sidewalk to work and back again, day in and day out. There are still others who do not know that the milk they buy in the store comes from a cow! While I am not advocating that we each buy a cow and a barn and become farmers, I am saying that we have lost much of value along the way. We make tiny compromises here, small sacrifices there, and before you know it, we are many times removed from the magical place we once lived and breathed as children—our own planet, the Earth.

We never do forget that youthful wisdom, however; for while we may *feel* disconnected, especially in the midst of our modern, industrial world, in reality we are not. The ancient rhythms of the seasons are not only universal, they are instinctive. The primeval drive that compels us to respond to the changing seasons still lives within each of us.

Our inseparable relationship to Mother Earth is nowhere more beautifully represented than in the Wheel of the Year. The Wheel of the Year is an ancient and sacred ritual calendar marking the Earth's changing seasons and the Sun's never-ending journey across the sky. This extraordinary calendar was begun by Witches in pre-Christian, proto-Celtic times and is observed by Witches today in its modern form. Each event marks a significant moment of change in the Earth and is rooted in one of the eight lunar and solar festivals of the ancient Celts.

The calendar is circular (as shown in the illustration on p. x) and includes as polar opposites on the eternal Wheel the following holidays: Samhain (pronounced *sow-en)* and Beltane, Imbolc and Lughnasadh (pronounced *loo-na-sa),* the Summer and Winter Solstices, and the Spring and Autumn Equinoxes. Though there is some debate over whether our Celtic ancestors celebrated the solstices and the equinoxes, these festivals are today generally accepted as important holidays on the Wheel of the Year. I personally believe the Celts honored both the solstices and the equinoxes, for how could a people so intimately tied to the Earth's cycles not acknowledge so profound an event as the Sun's changing heat and light? It's an absurd contention by so-called historians that the Celtic tribes, who were followers of the Old Religion, or Witchcraft—one of the oldest nature religions on the planet—failed to pay tribute to so obvious a change in course by the Sun. The ancient Celts, whether you choose to call them Witches, Druids, or pagans, were expert astronomers and engineers. Indeed, twentieth-century science is often involved in a game of "catch-up" with what we Witches call magic! Our Celtic Goddesses and Gods have known many "scientific facts" to be true since before the beginning of time.

While the solstices and equinoxes follow the path of the

Sun at its high, low, and median points, the lunar holidays of Samhain, Beltane, Imbolc, and Lughnasadh signified important agricultural and pastoral events to the ancient Celts. The two most important holidays, Samhain (October 31st) and Beltane (May 1st) divide the year into two parts, Winter and Summer. On Samhain, animal herds were brought into stockades for shelter and food for the winter, while on Beltane, the herds were driven outside to greening pastures. Imbolc (February 1st) marked the lactation period of ewes and cows, and Lughnasadh (August 1st) took place at the height of summer, the golden time in between harvests when competitions were held, and trial marriages were sometimes entered into for a year and a day.

Each holiday, or Sabbat, brings joy and good times along with deeply felt spiritual, cultural, and ecological meaning. Celebrated in three-day cycles, festivities for Celtic holidays carry on for three eagerly anticipated days encompassing the eve of, day of, and day after celebrations. For example, Beltane, which is technically May 1st, begins on April 30th and continues on into May 2nd.

While some of the Celtic festivals take place on the same day as their modern counterparts (Samhain coincides with Halloween; and Winter Solstice, or Yule, sometimes happens on the same day as Christmas), others do not. Celtic holidays coincide with dramatic moments of natural change in the Earth and Sky, and therefore all festivities take place during that time. One cannot celebrate the Spring Equinox, for example, as if it were a president's birthday or a bank holiday, moving it forward or backward in the week to accommodate a work schedule or to create a long weekend. When the Sun is at its median point in relation to the Earth, it is at its median point, whether it is a Wednesday or a Saturday. When we observe these eight great days, we are observing a particular alignment of space, energy, matter, and time.

It is important and beneficial both to ourselves and to our environment to take these eight days off from work, if we are able. If it is impossible, however, to break away from a job or project, there are many other ways to participate in or at least personally recognize our Mother's eight natural events. On a lunch break, you could walk through the Autumn leaves or simply sit in the cool shade of a tree. In the dead of Winter, venture outdoors to feel the snow and ice on your hands. Eight times a year, stop what you are doing for a moment to be respectful and mindful of your planet, your Mother, the Earth. What is she saying to you? Where are the planets, Moon, and stars at this point on the Wheel? How can I nurture and care for the Earth so that she in turn will care for me?

As a Witch, I take an active role in the changing of the seasons, helping to turn the Wheel. Just as other religions have standards or commandments one must follow, these eight points on the Wheel of the Year are our "commandments" or laws, and we must abide by them. You don't, however, have to change religions or even be a Witch to celebrate the eight holidays on the Wheel or to perform any of the rituals, spells, or meditations in this book. The Wheel is there for all to enjoy and cherish. The Earth will continue to spin and the seasons change. The question we each must ask ourselves is: "Will the Wheel continue to turn with or without *me?*"

By observing the Wheel of the Year, we are learning to respond and act toward the Earth, for She is always responding and acting toward us. She gives us clean or foul air to breathe, clear or poisoned water to drink, and rich or poor soil to till. The folly of our human family has been in thinking we could grow old without Her counsel.

Celebrate the Earth is a simple guide to help us reclaim the lost knowledge of our ancestors and the beauty and meaning of our planet's ancient peaceful balance. Just as a Witch's ritual progresses from a solemn to a joyous occasion, *Celebrate the Earth* emphasizes the importance of combining serious commitment to the environment with hope, fun, and enchantment.

The book is naturally divided into eight sections, one for each holiday. Each chapter is divided into three parts. Earth Magic offers sample rituals, herbcraft, spellcraft, magical stones, and lore about that particular holiday. Holiday Fare gives suggestions for what to serve at each point on the Wheel. I hope to impress upon the reader the magical qualities of food and food preparation and the importance of doing our best to eat regionally, especially during Wheel of the Year celebrations. Some of the recipes I've included hail from Celtic lands, while others do not. Although we may try, we can't always eat the foods of our ancestors. (It is difficult to find wild boar at the local market!) We should, however, take into account the region in which we live and try to buy foods not found in our area from their native sources. I come from New England and so use locally grown fruits and vegetables like apples and corn in many of my holiday meals. I also frequently enjoy oatmeal, but order it from Ireland, where oatmeal comes from originally. Where possible, I have provided the magical intentions of ingredients, but suggest you consult an herb dictionary for more elaborate explanations. The third section in each chapter, Ancient Activities, offers crafts and games passed down through many generations of Witch families, which are fun to take part in during the holiday season.

It is my hope that with this book each reader will explore our intriguing and provocative planet as if through a child's eyes, and once again experience the joy of these ancient

Celtic traditions. I encourage each of you to participate in the Wheel of the Year, and to believe in yourself and in the restorative powers that dwell within every human being. Now is the time to speculate and act upon the infinite connectedness of all things, the vision of universality. We must consider and nurture the radiant bloom of Witch wisdom within each of us, forever passing and forever present. I realize now that the powerful magic we possess is the answer to healing Mother Earth.

SAMHAIN
(October 31st)

★

Samhain (pronounced *sow-en)* is no doubt the most important, though least understood, of the ancient Celtic festivals. Unlike its modern counterparts of Halloween or All Hallows' Eve, the Witch holiday of Samhain has nothing to do with evil practices or horrific, ghoulish costumes. There are no poison apples or razor blades, no hatchet-faced masks or bloody stumps. *Witches do not have green faces!* (Although it feels like I've been saying this so long, I'm now blue in the face!) *Witches do not wear pointy hats!* Tall, pointed hats were simply the fashion of the day among the peasantry during the late Middle Ages. In ancient Celtic times, everybody was a Witch and everybody practiced Witchcraft. Witchcraft was and still is a living religion. It is in fact more than a religion. It is a way of life.

Samhain is a holiday infused with positive energy and filled with hope for our planet's future. With the icy, cold months of Winter about to begin, it is fitting that on every Samhain Eve the Morrighan, one of a triplicity of Celtic Goddesses with the power to give birth to a new land, celebrates her ritual union with the Dagda, the "Good God," one of the highest, most illustrious of Celtic Gods. The Morrighan is a Goddess of gigantic proportions, who is straddling the two sides of a river when She encounters the Dagda eating from a cauldron along the river's edge. Although She possesses a complexity of abilities both good and bad, the Morrighan's role on this night is to reaffirm life in the face of Winter's impending hardships and struggles.

To the ancient Celts, this great holiday divided the year into two seasons, Winter and Summer. Samhain is the day on which the Celtic New Year and Winter begin together, so it is a time for both beginnings and endings. On Samhain the ancient tribes celebrated the Celtic Feast of the Dead. Today we continue to honor the memories of our ancestors. This practice has directly influenced countless other religions and folk customs. All Souls' Day, on November 2nd, commemorates the Christian dead. On Samhain the veil between the worlds of spirit and matter is lifted and the living and dead are more likely to exchange psychic information. On All Souls' Day the barriers between this world and the next are said to be down and the dead are ominously able to return from their graves. Samhain is a much less frightening celebration. On Samhain Witches perform rituals to keep anything negative from the past—evil, harm, corruption, greed—out of the future. We cast spells to psychically contact our deceased forebears and retrieve ancient knowledge, thus preserving the great web that stretches through many generations of human families.

Samhain is a time for change and a time to look to the future. Today, as in the past, pagans dress for Samhain in a costume reflecting what we hope to be or achieve in the coming year. How we dress on Samhain is, in a manner of speaking, a Witch's New Year's resolution. If we want to be beautiful, we might dress as a butterfly or Faery Queen to ensure that our spiritual journey through life has power and sweetness; if we hope for prosperity and success, we might dress as a princess; or if we want to experience more confidence and strength, we could dress as a wolf or a bear.

Many of us are happy with ourselves, and so come dressed as we are to Samhain festivities.

The idea of trick-or-treating, though radically altered, is also descended from Witch tradition. In our celebrations, there is no trick, only treat. Witches pull no pranks and perform no mischief on Samhain Eve. After the rituals of the Magic Circle, we go not to houses of strangers but to the homes of friends to show off our costumes and sample treats.

Samhain is a mystical and enchanted night, when magic can be done to benefit our personal lives as well as our planet.

WITCH SOLIDARITY

The most impressive display of Witch solidarity is seen at the festivities for Samhain, more than at any other holiday on the Wheel of the Year. Each year more than three thousand Witches from around the globe come to Salem, Massachusetts, to take part in the candlelight vigil from Gallows Hill. The year 1992 marked the 300th anniversary of the Salem Witch trials, in which nineteen people were hanged and one man was pressed to death with stones. Witches in Salem today take issue with the fact that throughout the anniversary, the Mayor's Tercentennary Committee perpetuated the misuse of the word *Witch* in a blatant and disgraceful manner. In all of the publicity, displays, and museum exhibits, the committee used the word in the exact same way as their witch-hunting Puritan forefathers did. They equated the word *Witch* with "evil-doer" and "sinner," and would not allow the Witch community in Salem to accompany the incorrect definition with an honest and accurate one. A memorial was erected in honor of the victims of the Salem trials, which reads: I AM NO WITCH. I AM NOT GUILTY OF SUCH SIN. In other words, we are still letting our enemies define us. Furthermore, in order to erect the monument, the bodies of some of the earliest settlers were dug up at the Charter Street cemetery, but their gold and silver belt and shoe buckles were saved! This "sinful" action was fully authorized by the Tercentennary Committee. Whether those who were hung and killed were actually Witches or not, we thank them on Samhain for having suffered for our benefit. Witches must speak out against injustice and wrongdoing. We must unite if we are ever to practice openly and freely again.

EARTH MAGIC

The Samhain ritual keeps us steadfast in our understanding that human life parallels the changing of the seasons—that through death in Winter we pass on to new life in Spring. We honor the dead—those who came before us and who may have suffered for our benefit—but we also recognize the incredible change in the Earth from Summer to Winter.

In ancient times, ritual fires were kindled on sacred hilltops for the protection of the people and the land. The Samhain fires were lit at dusk, as opposed to the Beltane fires of May, which were lit at dawn. Many modern texts inaccurately interpret these bonfires as a means of ridding the land of Witches. The original purpose of a bonfire, however, was simply to destroy anything harmful or negative from the previous year. When the definition of *witch* became perverted over time to mean "evil," the intent and symbolism behind the ritual fires also became perverted. These fires were begun by Witches themselves, and were used in ceremonial rites for protection.

Before the widespread persecution of Witches during the Burning Times of the late Middle Ages, ritual fires were often built on sacred sites within circles of standing stones. During the Samhain ritual today, fire is used symbolically in our Magic Circle (see Appendix: Some Basic Elements of Witchcraft) to build a shield of protection and to light our path to good things in the future. On Samhain we perform rituals for strength and commitment to achieve our goals in the coming year.

While performing the Samhain ritual, it helps to remember not only that the veil between the living and the dead is thinnest at this time, but the veil between *all* worlds is vulnerable. In the Magic Circle, all Otherworlds are acknowledged. For example, each person possesses a realm that he or she creates and visits. It is a place where you alone own the palace and the land, a magically vivid interior landscape where you alone are sovereign. During the Samhain ritual, we visit this world in order to remove any obstacles or problems we may have placed in our paths. The personal clarity we seek in life is often touched upon and sometimes found in the murmured revelations and fluency of images of this powerful and emotional rite.

The Samhain ritual is also the time to project for beneficial change on Earth. Within the Magic Circle we do magic for favorable change in the larger community. Using our psychic abilities, we visually plant gardens and trees that we physically plant at Beltane in May. Thus it is that, to pagans, the dark of approaching Winter brings with it the seeds of new life in Spring.

Preparations

Deep golds, expiring scarlets, dark browns, and bronze are the predominant colors of late Autumn and the Samhain altar. The candles on the altar should be black, orange, white, silver, and gold. Black collects and absorbs light and keeps you warm. Orange represents the magic of fire as well as the remainder of fire in Autumn leaves. White sends out energy, and silver and gold represent the Moon and Sun, respectively. Candles should always be lit with altar matches (matches with no writing or advertising on the box). A stone indigenous to your region might be present on the altar as a symbol of the Earth. Because Samhain marks the completion of the third and final harvest, the meat harvest, an animal horn, feather, or talon might be placed on the altar as a power symbol. The crow is the Celtic totem animal of the Goddess Macha. A crow's feather, which is usually easier to find than an animal horn or claw, would be an appropriate Samhain representation of the Great Goddess.

For the ritual given below, you will need the following items (all of which can be found at Witch supply shops and mail-order catalogs listed in the Sources section of this book): a peyton, a ritual blade, or athame, a chalice filled with spring water, sea salt, Samhain incense, Protection Oil (see p. 29), an animal horn or antlers of a stag, wolf's hair from a live, shedding wolf, a swan feather, brass candleholders, one obsidian ball, one iron cauldron, one thurible (or incense burner), two crystals—one for incoming energy, placed on the left side of the altar, and one for outgoing energy, placed on the right side—two silver branch wands, and four different masks, one each representing the White Swan, Stag, Black Swan, and White Harte. A silver branch wand is a Faery wand and can be made from a branch that is painted or plated silver, usually about twenty-one inches long. There are seven silver bells, or Faery bells, tied on it in a row. If you cannot find or make the masks, you can use a picture of each as a representation.

In prepartion for Samhain we spend time alone, often days or hours before our ritual. Samhain is a time to speak to and explore your ancestors. By doing so we try to clear the air for the coming year. If, for example, one of your relatives has passed away, whether recently or long ago, on Samhain you might want to wear something that belonged to that person, perhaps a pin, a pair of cuff links, or a tie. Samhain can be a good time to deal with grief or resolve problems and obstacles that have limited you or hindered you in the previous year. Ask questions. Try to look to the coming year with a renewed strength and resolve.

The Celts did not view death in the way that many in our society do today. They believed in reincarnation and in the eternal circle of life-in-death and death-in-life represented by our pantheon of Goddesses and Gods. At Samhain, it sometimes helps to write down some of your thoughts and feelings about your ancestors or the death of close relatives or friends. I know that it has helped me in the past. Here are two examples from previous years of my contemplations about passing on from this world to the next.

> *O foul world of death and dying, that we cover with lace, trinkets, and coin to bide our time. What passion is spent in delusion of another world, or of not ending. What breath can spirit draw? Is it sweet? Is it unending?*

And:

> *Does the worried mind belong only to the living? . . . Hopefully. Is the invading spirit the process of thought?*

Can thought end? Hopefully the spirit races onward to another living body, and with it brings worry and thought, leaving the host body to vanish and decay at peace, to quiet, hearing not, seeing not, thinking not, blending into a place that is untroubled, more silent than the wings of an owl.

Two days before the ritual, contemplate the meaning of this time of year and the solemn ritual you are about to experience. This is the last harvest, so a sense of loss is imminent. We sit and think about the losses we have had in our lives. Ancestors, family, and loved ones who have already gone to Avalon, or Summerland, our holy city of milk and honey, are sorely missed. I often think of my mother and father around this time of year. I speak out loud to them. I sometimes spend several hours grieving at their loss, remembering the wonderful things, some sad things, and many things left unresolved between us. I know that, because the veil is thin between their world and mine at Samhain, together we can communicate our concerns, love, and happiness. I renew in my mind that I, too, will go to Avalon.

To prepare for the Samhain ritual, take a long, warm bath the night before. Add two tablespoons sea salt, which can be purchased at a gourmet food store, to the bath water and burn an incense of frankincense and myrrh. Light a white candle and set it on the edge of the tub, and turn on music that is nostalgic and reminds you of your ancestors or the ancient past. Soak in the tub and visualize yourself purifying your aura, body, and mind. Use soap with a scent that brings you back in time. After the bath lie down and count into an alpha state of consciousness (see p. 262) and switch your thinking to the coming new year, and to where and what you want to be in this coming year. Visualize yourself already there. Fall asleep with a deep remembrance of the past and a calming glimpse of your future.

Preparing for a ritual also means reflecting upon the astrological aspects of that particular day. For this you will need an astrological calendar, which can be purchased at any Witch supply shop or bookstore. On each holiday find the answers to the following questions: Where is the Moon? What are the aspects of the Moon? Is the Moon waning or waxing? What astrological signs are affecting the Sun's energy? How do these astrological signs affect my own sign and chart? These are questions to ask at all rituals. Knowing the nature of these energies creates a strong influence for the good when doing any ritual.

What to Wear

On Samhain, as on most Sabbats, we wear our black robes. To these we add jewelry and magical symbols to increase their power. Orange and gold, the fire colors of the Sun, are used at this time to attract sunlight to the Wheel of the Year. Some priestesses and priests wear a robe or costume to signify light or a very glittery robe or headdress to reflect light. Some wear stones or glitter on hands and face. Salem is alive with glittery costumed figures on Samhain night. Feathers trail from their headdresses and masks, and black capes unfurl in the Autumn breezes. Face painting is an old Celtic art we often practice on Sabbats. Adding glitter to the paint can be beautiful. Many Witches choose to be tattooed, which is also an ancient Celtic art. Of course, one needs to think twice or more about marking the body permanently, but tattooing was and is today considered by Witches to be your ticket to the Otherworld.

The Ritual

All the rituals given as examples in this book are meant for large groups of people. They are given as suggestions for you to adapt, scale down or up, or to trigger entirely new rites of your own. The following ritual is a collaboration between two covens, my own and the Coven of Akhellarre, which is presided over by Lady Zara, HPs, and Lord Azarel, HP. In 1990 I traveled to England for Samhain and asked Lady Zara and Lord Azarel to oversee the festivities at Gallows Hill in Salem, Massachusetts. I asked them to erect Tara in the Celtic manner in ritual. I then wrote some poetry to set the tone, and suggested the use of the Swan, Stag, and Dragon as totem animals in the rite. Lord Azarel suggested calling on the Four Cities of the Tuatha de Danaan, or "children of Dana," who are the Gods and Goddesses of our sacred Celtic heritage.

Before beginning, the High Priest and High Priestess name a second High Priest, to carry the masks of the White Swan and Stag, and three other High Priestesses—one to carry the masks of the Black Swan and White Harte, and two others to carry the silver branch wands.

> The High Priestess casts the circle with her wand, walking clockwise in a circle.
>
> High Priestess: *I cast around us now the circle of power, inviting all Spirits that are correct for this rite to be with us this Samhain night. Let this space be protected from all energies and forces that might come to do us harm. May the Goddess and God watch over us, their children, this Samhain night. So mote it be.*
>
> The High Priest holds a peyton with his left hand, points to the East, and moves clockwise.
>
> High Priest: *There are four cities that no mortal eye*

has seen but that the soul knows. These are Gorias, that is in the East; and Findias, that is in the South; and Murias, that is in the West; and Falias, that is in the North. The symbol of Falias is the stone of death, which is crowned with pale fire. The symbol of Gorias is the dividing sword. The symbol of Findias is a spear. And the symbol of Murias is a hollow that is filled with water and fading light.

White Swan: *From Gorias the glistening city of dawn, which captures the Sun's first ray, we conjure thus the Sword of Nuada, to keep all ill away. Nuada of the Silver Arm, protect this circle from all harm. So mote it be.*

Black Swan: *From the torchlit city of Findias with flickering flames so bright, we conjure thus the Spear of Lugh upon this Samhain night. By the power of Lugh Longhand let thy presence be at hand. So mote it be.*

Silver Wand #1: *From the sunken city of Murias beneath whose waves the Gods now dream, we conjure the Dagda's Cauldron with wealth our lives to teem. Blessed Lord of Plenty, let our cauldrons never be empty. So mote it be.*

Silver Wand #2: *From the frost-grown city of Falias with silver star-streaked skies, we conjure thus the Stone of Fail, powers of Earth arise. By Dana, the Lady of Earth, power fill this rounded girth. So mote it be.*

The two High Priestesses carrying the silver branches stand in the West and form an archway with their boughs. The High Priestess and High Priest presiding over the ceremony take their places to the Eastern side of the archway. The High Priest wearing the masks of the White Swan and Stag faces the North, and the High Priestess wearing the masks of the Black Swan and White Harte faces South.

High Priest: *Great Goddess, you have been the delight of every Faery knoll. You have been the darling of every goodly land. You have been a speckled salmon in a full pool, granting us wisdom. You have been a wiley red fox in the golden wood, seldom seen. Bright lady, speak unto us.*

Black Swan: *I have been a black swan with wings of ebony and eyes of jet.*

High Priestess (invoking): *Great God, you have been the might of sunlight warming our souls. You have been the Midsummer blaze round which we have danced. You have been a dragon before hosts at the onset, leading us to victory. You have been a golden lion with breath as sweet as summer hay. Bright lord, speak unto us.*

White Swan: *I have been a white swan with wings of ivory and eyes of sapphire.*

High Priest and High Priestess (with arms upraised, say together): *Sacred pair that were before the dawn of time and shall be till the twilight, like yoked Swans, transcend the Earthly Planes as we turn the Wheel from Summer to Winter, from Light to Dark. Transcend and be transformed by the silver branch of Avalon, the archway of eternity.*

The High Priest and High Priestess pass through the archway while the branch-bearers ring the bells by gently shaking the boughs. While they pass through the archway, the Black Swan changes masks to the White Harte and the White Swan changes masks to the Stag.

High Priest: *From Black Swan to White Harte and White Swan to Black Stag you shapeshift, taking on your Winter guises!*

High Priestess: *Dark Lord, you are a yellow-eyed wolf of the Great Forest, vigilant watcher and protector. You are a bearded ram that is spared from the knife, that the life of the flock goes on. Great God, speak unto us this sacred night.*

Stag: *I am the black stag of dark Midwinter, with antler of silver.*

High Priest: *Dark Lady, you are a dappled seal frolicking in the frothy Winter waves. You are a mother owl in a chill, hollowed oak with memories of warmer days. Great Goddess, speak unto us this sacred night!*

White Harte: *I am the White Harte of the icy wood. My presence bodes good fortune. Catch sight of me and you are blessed.*

The masks are removed.

High Priest and High Priestess: *On this night of Samhain, Summer's end, we greet the Winter, knowing full well that at bright Beltane we will be saying farewell. With this thought in mind, let us be Merry in spite of the growing icy chill. For in death is life, and in life is death and the Wheel is ever turning.*

The bells are knelled nine times for the Crone, and a projection spell is read.

Song: *Ye Witches hear these tidings. Now Samhain fires are burning. Come tread the round on sacred ground. The Sabbat Wheel is turning. Set your spirits free. Blessed be. By Earth, Air, Water, and Fire. Let no one fear who enters here, but fulfillment of desire.*

The High Priest heats the blade of the athame in the cauldron's flame, raising the cone of power. He plunges the blade into the chalice in the token great rite.

High Priest: *As chalice is to blade, as lance is to grail, as man is to woman, let their union bring blessedness, and love, and harmony, and fruitfulness. So mote it be.*

The Sabbat cakes are blessed and shared by the participants. As the participants speak, the High Priestess releases the quarters holding the peyton with her right hand and walks widdershins, or counterclockwise, facing first to the North, then West, South, and East.

Silver Branch #2: *By the powers of North, Stone of Fail, we release thee unto thy fair and native city of Falias. Go now in friendship and in peace as ye did come, but remember to return when next we do call. Go now, harming no one on thy way. In the name of Dana, we say Hail and Farewell.*

Silver Branch #1: *By the powers of the West, Cauldron of the Dagda, we release thee unto thy fair native city of Murias. Go now in friendship and in peace as ye did come, but remember to return when next we do call. Go now, harming no one on thy way. In the name of the Dagda, we say Hail and Farewell.*

White Harte: *By the powers of the South, Spear of Lugh, from the torch-lit city of Findias, we release you. Go now in friendship and in peace as you did come, but remember to return when next we do call. In the name of Lugh, Hail and Farewell.*

Stag: *By the powers of the East, the Sword of Nuada, City of Glistening Dawn, we release thee unto your fair city of Gorias in friendship and in peace, as ye did come, but remember to return when next we do call. Go now, harming no one on thy way. In the name of Nuada, we say Hail and Farewell.*

Magical Herbs

Herbs enhance many aspects of our lives; their uses range from medicinal and decorative to savory and aromatic. While it is laudable that we've finally come to our senses and, amid today's "herbal renaissance," rediscovered the many virtues of herbs, it is surprising to me that we've often forgotten or dismissed the magical potential of these remarkable plants.

Herbs, like everything in the universe, have an aura, an invisible charge of energy that radiates from within and without. This field of energy interacts with the light energy given off by the planets in our solar system. We say an herb is "ruled" by a certain planet or planets whose light energy is contained in the herb. Witches know how to use an herb's energy for magical purposes.

Before using herbs, it is important to charge them either in a Magic Circle or by holding the herb in your hand, going into an alpha state of consciousness (see p. 262), and visualizing what you want the herb to do. Because an herb has an aura, it interacts with the auras of other substances. By charging the herb, you cause or accelerate its interaction, thereby increasing its potency and facilitating its magical intent. Charged herbs not only work better in potions, philtres, and blends, but if they're edible, they taste better too!

At Samhain, the Sun's energy is being drawn into the Earth. We use herbs ruled by the Sun to bring the Sun's strength and warmth to us, but we also use many herbs ruled by the Earth. These are for grounding and stability.

On Samhain, rosemary holds a position of high esteem. Shakespeare wrote, in *Hamlet*, "There's rosemary, that's for remembrance." Because Samhain signifies the remembrance of our ancestors, we use rosemary frequently in our holiday decorations, Faery magic, and meals. In times past, bridal bouquets always included rosemary to remind the bride of the loving home she was leaving. The groom wore rosemary to remind him to be faithful. Rosemary was tossed onto coffins in funeral rites as a gesture of remembrance. On Samhain we sometimes braid rosemary into our hair for both remembrance and protection.

Mullein seeds also figure prominently during Samhain tide. Used for lighting torches, mullein is a grain that also feeds you well. Witches use mullein seeds in Samhain philtres and oils as a projection for abundance. Following is a list of herbs, seeds, plants, or flowers that work well during Samhain festivities:

- rosemary
- rue
- calendula
- sunflower petals and seeds
- pumpkin seeds
- mullein seeds
- turnip seeds
- apple leaf
- sage
- mushrooms
- wild ginseng
- wormwood
- tarragon
- bay leaf
- almond
- hazelnut
- passionflower
- pine needles
- nettle
- garlic
- hemlock cones
- mandrake root

Acorns also have a variety of uses during Samhain. Witches on Samhain sometimes present acorns to each other as gifts. During the Burning Times, giving someone an acorn was a secret means of telling that person you were a Witch. In addition to empowering your magic, acorns are symbols of protection, fertility, growth, and friendship, values we heartily embrace in the face of the long, cold winter months ahead. Acorns are the "fruits" of an oak tree, one of the many trees the ancient Celts regarded as sacred (see p. 267). Any magic can be done by asking a tree. Simply cast your Magic Circle and ask, in the name of the particular tree, whatever it is you seek. Acorns are also used in many Samhain philtres, oils, and incense.

Philtres, Incense, and Oils

A philtre can be a blend of dried herbs or a mixture of herbs, stones, or feathers—anything that you've charged with a magical mission and can be carried with you in a small magic bag. Incense is a mixture of ingredients using an aromatic gum or resin as a base and is meant to be burned. Witches use incense in ritual either to purify the air or to release certain energies into the air and light. Oils are used in ritual to anoint candles, and can be worn as a magical perfume or used as ingredients in a spell or philtre.

Using your imagination to experiment with ingredients transports you to a fantastic land of unique blends and amazing results. One pinch sea salt, two parts acorn oil, hair of wolf! Concocting a brew or blend to create a philtre, incense, or oil fills one with a childlike anticipation of what might be. Living by magic, as children do, is exciting.

On Samhain, there is an extra edge or bite in the air that will add to the adventures you'll find in the kitchen. The wind carries magic with it, and the crisp air and clean clouds of Autumn make it seem like anything is possible when it comes to creativity.

Following are a few suggestions of some of my favorite Samhain blends, but these are merely suggestions. Don't be afraid to add a little bit more or less of this or that to come up with some terrific concoctions of your own.

SACRED OAK OIL

broken-up oak leaves
grape oil (or sunflower oil)
pinch sea salt
one acorn

Blend ingredients and simmer on low heat in an enamel pan. Remove from burner and let cool. Place it in a small bottle or bowl that will only be used to charge and anoint items such as candles in your Magic Circle. To charge the oil itself, bring it into your Magic Circle or sacred space.

PROTECTION OIL

1 dram patchouli oil
1 dram each frankincense and myrrh
1 tsp. broken pieces of mandrake root
3 heaping tsp. coarse sea salt

MACHA PHILTRE

pine needles
mushrooms
rosemary
sunflower petals
sage
apple leaves

At Samhain, Macha appears in the Crone aspect of the Triple Goddess. Her totem animal is the Crow. Carry this philtre in an orange or black magic bag, and tie a crow feather to it if you'd like to represent her. Add 3 drops of Sacred Oak Oil to bind the philtre's ingredients.

SAMHAIN INCENSE

Blend 1 tablespoon of each of the following:

nettle	*calendula*
bay leaf	*a little bit of oak leaf*
tarragon	*2 drops frankincense*
sage	*or myrrh*

Place all ingredients in a bowl only to be used for magical purposes. The frankincense or myrrh is a resin used to bind the ingredients and retain scent. Burn in a thurible on an instant-light charcoal.

MACHA OIL

2 drams grapeseed oil	*2 dried mushrooms*
1 dram hemlock oil	*1 crow feather*
1 dram pine oil	

Charge all ingredients in a circle or sacred space. Blend oils and mushrooms. To call on Macha, dip the crow feather into the oil blend three times.

Magical Stones

Stones are perfect evidence that the tools of magic are all around us. Stones are forces of nature found in your own backyard. Gems, crystals, metals, or any stones indigenous to your area possess magical power and energy that Witches find especially useful on Samhain.

Often on Samhain we use black obsidian in rituals and spells. Black obsidian is a catalyst for what I call "instant magic." It is a stone with the power to make things change in any direction, from good to bad, for example, or from chaos to clarity. On Samhain we first neutralize the stone's energy and then recharge it to cause only positive change.

On Samhain Witches often wear black and gold jewelry. Black, a composite of all colors of the spectrum, retains light and warms you. We might wear jewelry made from jet, obsidian, or smoky quartz. We never wear black onyx, however, because onyx scatters your energy. Only Capricorns can handle the magical power that comes from wearing onyx. Clear quartz crystal is used on each holiday on the Wheel of the Year to empower and enhance your magic.

Stones, metals, crystals, and gems for Samhain include:

granite	gold
marble	diamond
sandstone	iron
smoky quartz	steel
clear quartz	ruby
obsidian	pyrite
jet	garnet
amber	hematite
onyx (Capricorns only!)	brass

Any of these can be used as an amulet for protection or for drawing in the energy of the Sun or the stabilizing aspects of the Earth.

Magical Spells

Spells are prayers Witches send out into the universe to effect beneficial change. They are mental projections we either speak, write, or think. In my own coven, we write down spells, think about them, and read them aloud before actually casting a spell in a Magic Circle. Wording your spell correctly is important. Words are powerful instruments in and of themselves. In the form of a spell, cast in the magical setting of a Witch's Circle, they wield an ineffable strength. Before casting a spell, make sure you know what you're asking for, because once you ask for it, you're going to get it. I write spells on parchment or loose, unlined, unbonded sheets four to five inches in size. Use recycled paper for everything except for writing spells, because whatever was written there before will conflict with the spell you are writing. Any spell can be cast using three ingredients or herbs. The more ingredients you use, however, the more powerful the energies raised.

Spells are also ways Witches use to protect themselves through magic. There is no doubt that harm, hardship, suffering, and struggle exist in the world, but Witches take responsibility for their own safety. We reject the belief that our lives are determined by fate or evil forces beyond our understanding. Nor do we believe that our lot in life is retribution for some evil deed we may have committed in a past life. Witches know how to defend themselves without causing harm to others. The bottom line is, we all have to live with what we create. Witches believe that whatever spell we cast out into the universe comes back to us three times; therefore, emotions like greed, jealousy, envy, or vengeance are counterproductive in magic. Instead we practice an "active resistance" against using magic for harm. We cast protection spells and know how to neutralize harm. After each spell we ask that it is "correct and for the good of all." Above all else, the Witches' Credo states: "Do what you will, and it harm none."

Casting protection spells and neutralizing harm can be practiced at any time on the Wheel of the Year, but

Samhain, the dark half of the year, is often a good time to shore up your confidence and security.

SAMHAIN PROTECTION SPELL

You will need:

1 black candle
1 white candle
1 peyton
1 chalice
1 four-inch square of paper
1 black pen
1 ash pot
1 thurible
1 instant-light charcoal
wolf's hair from a live, shedding wolf
1 swan feather or crow feather
1 picture of a stag
1 orange ribbon, 3 feet long
1 black ribbon, 3 feet long
1 black magic bag or 4-inch square of black fabric
1 small bottle with a lid or cork
13 inches of black cord or string
Protection Oil (see p. 29)
Samhain Incense (see p. 30)

Wear a black robe and pentacle. Anoint yourself with Protection Oil before setting the altar. Set the altar in Samhain fashion, adding tools listed above. Face the altar North so that you stand facing North. After anointing the wand with Protection Oil, cast the circle with your wand three times clockwise. Say:

This circle will protect me from all positive and negative energies and forces that may come to do me harm. So mote it be. I cast a ring of Earth, one of Air, one of Water, one of Fire, and one of crystal.

In your magic third eye, envision five rings around your

circle. Step in front or sit in front of your altar, raise your hands to the sky and say:

I call into this sacred space the most perfect, balanced energies of the cosmos. I ask that they are correct and for all in this circle. So mote it be.

Anoint candles with Protection Oil and Samhain Incense. Touch the black candle and say: *I draw into this circle the God and Goddess. Blessed are the ancient ones. Come and abide with me to cast this spell.*

Touch the white candle and say: *I charge this candle to send out into the cosmos my spell to come to be—and it only—please the God and Goddess. So mote it be.*

Light both candles, anoint your ritual blade handle with one drop of Protection oil (only one drop!). Hold the blade to the sky upward over the chalice of water and say: *As chalice is to blade, as lance is to grail, as man is to woman, their union brings blessedness.*

Then put the blade into the chalice and stir the chalice three times, saying: *I charge this chalice with the power of the Goddess and God. So mote it be.*

Then lift the cup and drink the energy of the Goddess and God. Feel the cool water and magical power trickle down inside your body. Visualize the Goddess and God standing to your left and right, their auras mingled with yours.

Light the charcoal and sprinkle Samhain Incense on it. Take your pen and write: "I ask the Gods and Goddesses to protect me, my family, coven, animals, home, and friends from any evil thought, actions, or deeds of others. I ask that we all be placed in your shield of protection. So mote it be. I ask that this be correct and for the good of all."

Sprinkle more incense on the charcoal and smudge the spell by passing the paper through the smoke of the incense. Open the ash pot. Light the spell on fire by touching it to the black and then the white candle. Place it in the ash pot to burn. When the flames are out, raise your hands to send the spell out into the cosmos to come to be.

Hold all the other objects in your hands and charge them for protection. In your magic bag place the wolf's hair, Samhain Incense, one drop of Protection Oil, and crystal. When your spell is done, you may wear the bag or hang it in your home or office or car. Charge the ribbons and wear them or tie them to things that need protection. Tie the feathers to the magic bag or to the ribbons.

Undo the circle by circling around counterclockwise and saying: *This circle is undone but not broken.*

SAMHAIN NEW YEAR SPELL

Cast your circle and say:

I speak for all that attend, as High Priestess, sovereign of my magical time and space. I ask the Goddess and God to grant me: a bright and prosperous New Year, the wisdom of my ancestors and my past to be used in a correct way, that my spirit be filled with gratitude to our Lady and Lord, that I heal myself, the world, and all in it great and small—that Mother Earth be healed, the air clean, the water pure, and the Earth rich. I ask for clarity and harmony for all. So mote it be.

Samhain marks the completion of the third and final harvest on the Wheel of the Year—the meat harvest. In ancient times on this night, animals with the best chance of surviving the Winter were rounded up and billeted in stockades. The rest were slaughtered. What was not eaten at the Samhain feast was saved—either dried, cured, or smoked for later use during the colder months.

To the ancient tribes the killing and eating of an animal was by no means a senseless or gratuitous act. On the rare occasion when we had to fell an animal, we placed it upon an altar. With great ceremony and solemn ritual we would give thanks to the Goddess and God for exchanging life for life. I reject the idea that the Celts practiced animal—much less human—sacrifices at such gatherings to the extent that many modern texts propose. The so-called evidence carries with it a great deal of speculation about a time so long ago that time as we know it did not exist. Too much emphasis is placed on this aspect of Celtic history in an attempt, I believe, by naysayers and religious zealots to paint a one-dimensional portrait of Witches as evil-doers.

Today we honor the Celtic wisdom in regarding animal life as sacred by representing the power of the animal spirit on our altars and by acknowledging during the feast the supremacy of compassion. We give thanks to the Goddess —our Mother, the Earth—for her bounty, and realize that the meat or fish or fowl we are about to enjoy once had a body and a spirit attached.

HOLIDAY FARE

The Wiccan tradition embraces a principle of caring that demands we behave in a compassionate way to all other living beings.

Samhain offers some of the most delicious and inviting aromas of all the pagan holidays. From pumpkin breads and apple pies to roast pork and chicken soup, Samhain's Feast of Morrighan is a coveted ticket in the town of Salem for its nourishing, healing, and enchanted qualities. One year we decorated a great hall in Faeryland splendor with crystals, ribbons, and baskets of fruit and corn. A giant centerpiece of moss and cobwebs graced our long dining tables and a Celtic harpist filled the air with beautiful music. Decorate for your Samhain supper using fall colors and herbs, stones, fruits, and vegetables commonly found in your area around this time of year.

Here are some suggestions for what to serve at a Samhain meal.

THE FEAST OF MORRIGHAN

Mulled Cider with Spices
Pumpkin Bread
Chicken Soup à la Cabot in Pumpkin Shells
Roast Pork with Rosemary and Mint
Oven-roasted Red Potatoes and Apples
Candy Kelly's Wheel of the Year Sabbat Cakes

MULLED CIDER WITH SPICES

4–5 cups apple cider
3–4 cloves
2 sticks cinnamon

In a large saucepan heat cider, but do not boil. Serve in a large cauldron.

PUMPKIN BREAD

2 cups pumpkin, canned or cooked
1 cup melted butter or margarine, lightly salted
3/4 cup water
4 eggs
3 2/3 cups flour
2 1/4 cups sugar
1 1/2 tsp. salt
1 tsp. nutmeg
2 tsp. cinnamon

2 tsp. baking soda
1 cup raisins
1 cup walnuts, chopped

Blend pumpkin, butter, water, and eggs until mixed. Add flour, sugar, salt, nutmeg, cinnamon, and baking soda. Then add raisins and nuts. Form loaf in greased and floured loaf pans. Bake at 350° F for 1 hour or until top is golden brown.

CHICKEN SOUP À LA CABOT IN PUMPKIN SHELLS

Before preparing soup, cut out four quart-sized pumpkins, and one large three-quart-sized pumpkin to use as bowls and soup tureen. Chill in refrigerator until soup is ready to be poured.

TO MAKE THE SOUP:

3 qt. chicken broth
4 boned and skinned chicken breasts, cubed
2 cups pureed pumpkin
2 large onions, chopped
2–4 celery stalks, chopped fine
2 large carrots
2 pinches dried tarragon
1 clove garlic
½ tsp. salt

Add all ingredients except herbs and salt to pot. Slow simmer for 30 minutes, then add herbs and salt. Slow simmer for about 1 hour or until chicken is tender. Pour soup carefully into pumpkin tureen and bowls when ready to serve.

ROAST PORK WITH ROSEMARY AND MINT

Pork was considered a sacred source of nourishment to the Celts. Certain parts of the pig were given at feasts to honor those who performed well in battle and leadership.

roast pork loin
1 clove garlic, cut into thin slivers
fresh rosemary sprigs cut into 2-inch lengths
fresh mint sprigs (reserve 4 leaves for garnish)

Preheat oven to 450° F. Make small slits all over pork, and insert garlic slivers. Rub well with some sprigs of rosemary and mint. Place on a rack, fat side up, and put in oven, reducing heat to 350° F. Roast uncovered, figuring 35 minutes to the pound. Near end of roasting, add some extra sprigs of rosemary and mint, taking care not to scorch the herbs. Drain off fat, boil drippings to reduce, and strain. Keep warm and serve in a sauceboat.

OVEN-ROASTED RED POTATOES AND APPLES

6–8 red russet potatoes
6–8 apples
2 tbs. shortening

Parboil potatoes. Rub skins in shortening and place in roasting pan alongside apples. Roast at 350° F for 30 minutes.

CANDY KELLY'S WHEEL OF THE YEAR SABBAT CAKES

This is the recipe we use to make the cakes called for during all Sabbat rituals on the Wheel of the Year.

½ cup butter
¼ cup shortening
1 cup sugar
2 eggs
1½ tbs. honey
1 tsp. each vanilla extract, white wine, cinnamon, almond extract
1 tsp. each baking powder and salt
2½ to 3 cups flour
2 tbs. oats

Mix butter and shortening and melt. Add sugar, eggs, honey, vanilla, wine, cinnamon, and almond. In a separate bowl, blend baking powder, salt, flour, and oats. Combine dry ingredients with wet. Refrigerate for 1 hour. Roll out dough onto a floured board. Cut with crescent-shaped cookie cutter or roll dough into balls and stamp with star-shaped cookie stamp. Place on an ungreased cookie sheet. Bake at 350° F for 6 to 8 minutes or until golden brown.

ANCIENT ACTIVITIES

There are so many memorable traditions associated with modern-day Halloween fun—from carving jack-o'-lanterns and making costumes to bobbing for apples and trick-or-treating—that began with pagan practices. Witches dress up on Samhain, but not in scary costumes. Samhain is our New Year. In our tradition we dress up in costumes that reflect what we hope or wish for in the coming year. The practice of cutting faces or symbols in pumpkins or gourds is also a Witch tradition. Jack-o'-lanterns, as they became known, were a practical means of lighting your way in the dark, and to keep animals in the forest at bay. Following are a few other treasured and time-honored Witch customs that will widen your scope of holiday fun.

MAKING A WITCH'S CORD

The meaning and origins of Celtic knotwork are as intricate and mysterious as the knots themselves. A Witch's cord is an excellent example of a Celtic knot. It can be as simple as three strands of cord braided together or as intricate as the most elaborate Celtic knot. There are books of patterns of Celtic knots that can be purchased at bookshops specializing in Celtic mythology and history or through Witch mail-order supply sources.

Witch's cords are beautiful and make lovely gifts or home decorations. On Samhain, your Witch's cord should be an expression of what you wish or hope for in the coming year. To make a simple one you'll need three strands of black, white, and gold ribbon or silk cord, each about three feet in length. Fold one end down about five inches and tie together in a knot, making a loop so cord can be hung from a doorway or wall. Braid the three strands together, reciting things you hope to bring into the future. Then tie a knot. Make at least three knots on the tail. On the cord hang herbs, potions, a magical piece of wood. A magic bag or philtre containing wolf's hair should always be included on a Witch's cord for Samhain, because wolf's hair is for protection. Wolf's hair should always be from a live and shedding wolf. This can be obtained from Witch supply shops or from animal preserves that keep wolves (see Sources). But be creative. Use your imagination. Hang a talisman, perhaps, or an earring you've lost the mate to, or a token of remembrance from a loved one. All cords or Celtic knots are little spells cast out into the universe, so anything that has some meaning for you would be appropriate to add.

Finding a Wand

Samhain is a good time to look for a magic wand. The air is crisp and clear, but it is still not so bitterly cold we cannot venture out-of-doors. There were many kinds of wood that the Celts regarded as sacred or magical. These include oak, holly, ash, rowan, birch, hazel, elm, hawthorn, and willow. Although any of these can be used as a wand, hazel wood is most popular. Hazel has strong magical power. The hazelnut represents all wisdom. Any wood that has been struck by lightning is infinitely more desirable and powerful for a wand. Wood struck by lightning contains an electrical charge. You can actually feel the difference in the wood. Leaves often stay alive on a lightning-struck branch even though it has been cut down. I have branches from the oldest living oaks in England, given to me by an Arch Druid who has long since passed away. These are Druid oaks, gog and magog, or male and female. Their leaves are still green and I've had them for over ten years. When you've found your wand and cut the branch, you must thank the tree and the Faeries and the Goddess and God for their gift. During this time of year, do not let the branch touch the ground, lest its energies and powers return to the Earth.

MAKING CANDLES

Witches know how quickly bright things can turn to darkness. The deceptively modest flame of the candle has great importance in our magic. Where else in Nature does physical matter turn so simply first to pure flame and next to light? Like humans, candles have both a physical and a spiritual presence. In ancient times candles were usually made during the meat harvest, on Samhain, when there was fat to be had for tallow. I usually make my own candles near Samhain. In Summer, at Lughnasadh, I use beeswax to seal jars used in canning fresh fruits, vegetables, and herbs for Winter.

To make a candle, you'll need paraffin or beeswax, any size milk carton you choose, a pencil, a wick or piece of string, and a crayon in any color you like. In a double boiler, melt the wax slowly over very low heat. Add the crayon and also melt. While the wax and crayon are melting, tie the wick or string to the center of a pencil and suspend across the open square mouth of the milk carton. When the wax is melted, slowly and carefully pour it into the milk carton mold. (It is a good idea to place the milk carton in a pan to catch anything that may drip over.) When the wax is hardened, tear away the carton. You can make your candle more interesting and magical by adding one or two crystals, a tiny pinch or leaf from a favorite herb, or a tiny spell written on parchment. To do this, pour wax only one quarter of the way into the carton. Then add your herbs or crystals or spell, gently placing them around the edges using another pencil. Pour a little more wax and add another crystal, herb, or tiny spell, and so on until you fill the carton. If you want to give a lacy look to the candle, pour the wax over a few ice cubes in the bottom of the carton, before adding your magical items.

Faery Magic

To the ancient Celts, the Faery world or the *sidhe* (pronounced *she)* was a real place, a magical Otherworld or time outside of time, made up of a race of gifted people. All Celts have Faery blood, even today. The Faeries dwell in the Faery mounds or hilltops, and we often encounter them at sacred junctures, usually magical places on Earth that are actually seams between the worlds.

The Faeries were originally our Goddesses and Gods. They are the eternal Tuatha de Danaan, or "children of Dana," the Mother of us all. Over time, as Witches were persecuted and the Old Religion demeaned and degraded, our sacred Goddesses and Gods were reduced in status to become "fairies" or thought of as mythical, superstitious beings, much like Hollywood's Tinkerbell. Although many use the word *faery* in a derogatory manner even today, Witches turn its meaning around and use it proudly as a badge of integrity, strength, and magic. For as W. Y. Evans-Wentz states in his book *The Fairy Faith in Celtic Countries,* "It is only men who fear the curse of the Christians; the Faery folk regard it not."

During each holiday on the Wheel of the Year we should do Faery magic or rather do *something* to psychically receive messages. Try to see what you can see. Try to discover what has been and what is going to be. Faery magic is fun and intriguing.

We live in an age of information. On Samhain, it is important to remember that too much information sinks the boat of wonder and surprise. Samhain, above all, is a time to build on your imagination. Let yourself feel in your bones what it is to wonder and pretend. Everything we take part in on Samhain appeals to a sense of mystery and magic. As Albert Einstein once wrote: "The most beautiful experience we can have is the mysterious. It is the fundamental emotion which stands at the cradle of all true art and true science." Wiccans have known this to be true for untold centuries. Only when we see the world as a mysterious, strange, and magical place will we be curious about what makes it work and run and breathe. Samhain enchantment lights the fire of science with a healthy dose of wonder and surprise. Make no mistake: on this night, magic is in the air.

Fortune-telling is a favorite activity on Samhain. Communication between the living and the dead is most favorable at this time, and so we often wonder about our future, seeking answers to questions that lie ahead. There are so many fun ways to participate in fortune-telling that have been passed down through the ages and between the worlds. Peel an apple and throw the skin over your left shoulder. Whatever letter shape the skin forms is said to be the initial of the person you will marry. Another says that if you roast two nuts on the fire and they burn quietly, you'll soon be married. Scrying, or mirror gazing, is another favorite way for Witches to ascertain the future.

THE MAGIC MIRROR

Seeing your own reflection in a mirror in a meditative state is in effect like looking through a doorway to the Faery world. The mirror can be either hand held or on the wall. A mirror used for scrying should only be used for that purpose. Turn down the lights, light a candle or two, and count down into alpha or use the instant alpha trigger, crossing the fingers (see Appendix). See what you see. You can also dress up a Samhain scrying mirror by trimming it in crow feathers or by gluing stones used on Samhain around the edges. You can also make your own mirror. Buy a square of glass and glue it to a piece of black cardboard. Decorate the mirror by gluing a Witch's cord of orange and black around the rim, adding stones like smoky quartz or pyrite, and crow feathers or a magic bag of wolf's hair. Put your mirror on a plate stand to make it easier to scry. Drape black velvet over the mirror so no one else gazes into it. The magic mirror appeals to Samhain's deepest sense of mystery and magic. Have fun with it, be curious, and be willing to be surprised.

Aisling Cake

Baking fortune-telling charms into cakes or breads is an age-old Celtic tradition that used to be a part of every Samhain festival. I call my cakes Aisling cakes because Aislings are Faeries who bring us what we ask for. Wash and scrub the items to be used inside the cake. Usually I do not bake these inside the cake, but insert them later, covering them with frosting either on top of the cake or inside the layers. Baking the items can sometimes ruin them and ruin your cake. A large turkey bone, whether the thigh or the heavy bone from the wing, is essential to any good Aisling Cake. The turkey bone means you'll have to scry into the past to see your future. In other words, you'll have to look for a sign from your ancestors. Other items I use include a coin, for wealth; a ring, for marriage; a tiny doll, for birth; or a crystal. (Do not bake a crystal into the cake, insert it after baking.) As each person takes a slice, he says the following:

Aisling! Aisling!
Small friend, powerful Old
Bring to me a fortune told!

YULE

Winter Solstice
(around December 22nd)

★

The Yuletide season provides us with an ideal opportunity to reflect upon the ancient Welsh myth of Bran the Blessed, a vivid and compassionate tale that embodies the Wiccan values of giving, light, and rebirth. Bran's story is one of royal responsibility and great personal sacrifice, conciliation, and a king's love for his people and the land. In Celtic mythology a king or hero is considered protector or champion of the land. If he does not meet his obligations to the Goddess, Mother Earth, the land itself turns against him. Bran's myth is a story about how to be a good king.

Bran's sister, Branwen, is Goddess of the Land, and as such, She is Bran's reason for being. As Faery King and Guardian of the Cauldron of Rebirth, Bran is committed to his role as champion of Her cause. The Cauldron of Rebirth, originally from Ireland, has the power to bring dead warriors back to life and is a symbol of the law and power of the land. In the story Branwen marries Matholwch, the King of Ireland, in order to form a bond between Britain and Ireland. Branwen's brother, however, is upset by the marriage and kills all of Matholwch's horses. Bran replaces the horses, but Matholwch is not satisfied. In order to heal the breach, Bran must also give Matholwch the Cauldron of Rebirth. Despite so generous a gift, Matholwch is still not appeased. He mistreats Bran's sister so badly, Bran must

march into Ireland to save Her. To prevent his arrival, Matholwch burns the bridge leading across the Shannon River. But Bran shapeshifts into a giant and acts as his own bridge, carrying his men on his enormous shoulders through the sea. Thus, we find in Bran's story the important line, which serves as a lesson to all future leaders, "He who would be chief, let him make himself a bridge."

Without the Cauldron of Rebirth, Bran's forces are defeated and Bran is wounded. He orders his own beheading and while his men transport his head to be buried in the White Tower of London, Bran teaches his people everything he has learned from the Goddess's Cauldron of Rebirth, passing on his wisdom to all future generations. This image of Bran's head is one of many examples found in Celtic mythology and Witchcraft of the skull as a symbol of power and wisdom. The skull is not something to be feared. Modern Witches will often wear a skull as jewelry symbolizing the house of the brain.

Winter Solstice marks a point of dramatic natural change on Earth. This is simultaneously a time of balance and change. In its journey across the sky, the Sun, on Yule, is at its most southeastern point over the Tropic of Capricorn in the northern hemisphere and has no apparent northward or southward motion. Winter Solstice marks the longest night and the shortest day of the year. From this point on, the Sun rises earlier and earlier, each time adding a little more of His light and warmth to the cold and silent days of Winter. On Yule we honor the Goddess, Mother Earth, for giving birth to the Sun once more. Just as She draws the light within Her womb during the darkest time of the year, from Samhain to Yule, so does She create the light at Winter Solstice.

As with each movement of the Wheel, Witches perceive

the natural changes in the Earth as a pantheon of intriguing and passionate deities. At Yule the two God themes of death and rebirth coincide. The Holly King, retainer of light, who has symbolized death and darkness since Samhain, is vanquished by the rebirth of the Oak King, who symbolizes life. The holly and oak are two of the many trees sacred to the Celts (see p. 267). In the Yule ritual it is the job of the priestess, by invoking the Goddess in the Magic Circle, to give birth to the Sun. The Goddess possesses the eternal return of life that we witness and experience in every season on Earth. She is always Maiden, Mother, and Crone. By caring for and nurturing the Goddess, we care for and nurture ourselves.

Yule is a good time of year to think about what we learn from Bran's myth. This is a magical moment on the ever-turning Wheel: like Bran's story, it is full of heart and passion, lightness and gravity, hope and realism. Colors seem brighter on Yule; memory sharper, sweeter, warm, and shadowed as we begin again to see with a child's eyes our dreams and pictures in the flames. With warmth and brightness, the red heart of a Winter fire welcomes us in from cold nights of rustling firs and snowcapped fences. This is the time when we reflect on the unconquerable human spirit that the story of Branwen and Bran represents. We seek the sacredness of the whole, the oneness of all in the universe. We experience a tremendous soul-hunger.

I believe Yule, more than any other moment on the Wheel of the Year, is indicative of the unity of the Wiccan tradition. The beauty of the Old Religion is that it recognizes the interconnected nature of all existence. Wicca's aim is not to storm the sacred centers of our heritage by debunking other faiths, but to understand, nurture, and enjoy the special relationship that connects our modern holidays to our ancient, still vital traditions. While I do not believe it is possible to be a Catholic Witch any more than it is possible to be a Buddhist Baptist, Witchcraft respects all faiths. You are not a Witch, however, until you participate in a Witch tradition and adopt it as your religion. Many people are of different faiths but dedicated to the study of Witchcraft. Especially around Yule, we desire to cherish the best of all we have, and to seek out and acknowledge what is of great value in others. Yule is an awakening and a thankfulness for our knowledge of and connection to the Wheel of the Year.

MAGIC AT WILL

So many people want magic in their lives, but are afraid even to ask. When I look at modern religion today, it sadly becomes apparent to me that somewhere along the way the practice of religion in general went from something within the people's grasp to something beyond their reach. In Witchcraft, everyone is able to speak and communicate with the Gods and Goddesses. There is no hierarchy, and no single person acting as a link or pontificator between you and your deity. I believe that when people gave up this control, whether freely or by force, they were being robbed of their spirituality. Practicing the Craft is a turning away from loneliness and separation and a return to peace and integration with oneself and one's planet. I believe that in matters of religion your interpretive choices are and should be an utterly personal matter. Magic at will is about taking control of your own life. It is about being able to develop and use the psychic abilities that each of us is born with to work for your benefit. Of course, along with the power of magic comes a great deal of responsibility. The ancient tribes were not afraid of this. As the insidious attack on the religion of Witchcraft grew, people were persecuted for having these abilities. They were blamed for being able to shapeshift into other forms. The Goddesses and Gods were demeaned and made to look bad until they diminished in status to become the Faery folk. And now, so many of us are left with no religion at all. In Salem, people come to me all the time from all over the world to tell me there is something missing in their lives. They feel desperate and disconnected. They are watchers instead of doers. Their lives are stale. They feel out of control, but they're not sure why. Each feels exactly the way one feels when he's been robbed. Magic at will is about taking back that which was stolen.

EARTH MAGIC

The Yule ritual is a warmly memorable and enriching experience that helps to reconnect us to the spiritual and life-affirming essence of this magical holiday. In ritual, our Magic Circle is a sacred space where we create a world between worlds, a place where we alone rule. On Yule, in our mind's eye, we might want to travel to the land of the Snow Queen and Yule King. We might envision snowflakes dusting the ground like diamonds aglow on hillsides and meadows. We may want to rest inside the great hall of our mind's palace, where there is an enormous warm hearth to enjoy. The Yule ritual is a partnership of empowerment that breathes with the wind like fire, an odyssey to the heights of spiritual joy and wonder. We gather together on Yule to renew, celebrate, and see through innocent eyes.

Preparations

The altar on Yule is akin to a waking dream in the Faery world. Trimmed in the glossy green leaves and scarlet red berries of holly and ivy, silver crystals and golden cones of candlelight spread a gentle radiance that becomes strangely powerful and luminous. Gazing at the flames and modest wisps of spirit-smoke, one wonders at the transformations fire can produce. To set up the Yule altar, in addition to the standard black and white candles, bring one each of red, green, silver, and gold. These are the shades of Winter Solstice, representing fire, flora, the Sun, and the Moon, respectively. Drape the altar in a red cloth and trim with pinecones, evergreen boughs, and mistletoe. For the following ritual, you will also need a peyton, charcoal, a thurible, Winter Solstice Incense, Yule Oil (see p. 62 for both recipes), a gold ring, a chalice filled with spring water, and a ritual blade. We also bring two Yule logs, one from the year before and one for the coming year.

What to Wear

The High Priestess on Yule wears classic robes of red, green, or black. Our robes for Winter Solstice are red velvet, trimmed in dark hunter-green and cuffed with gold bells. A huge, long hood tipped with a gold bell hangs down the back. In the Magic Circle we name a Holly King, who wears a red cape and a crown of equal parts oak leaves and holly. We also name a Snow Queen, who wears a white cape and a glistening crown, and a Father Winter, who has a long white beard and wears a red-trimmed robe and crown of holly berries. These are positions of great honor. We try to choose young people or couples from our coven who enjoy children and the magic and kindness of Yule.

The Ritual

I always look forward to the gathering of the Witches in Salem on Yule, in anticipation of our magic rites. This is a time for laughter and the wonderful sounds and energy of children playing, singing, and dancing. We as a community get together to make or buy gifts for Father Winter to give. Our homes are decorated, and if we are going to a hall, the whole community joins in to help plan the celebration and make the Yuletide feast.

During Winter we tend to do most things indoors. Before the Winter Solstice ritual, I suggest finding a place to stroll or to enjoy the outside world, perhaps a rocky beach or even a park or garden. Try to find different kinds of birds, animals, and trees and see what messages they bring. Listen to the music in the wind. In one story passed down to us from the ancients, Hearne, the Stag of Seven Tines and God of the Woods, speaks of hearing the bark of a fox. It is good luck, according to the story, to meet a single fox on a winter night, but not so good to meet several. Upon learning this, one of my students on a cold wintry night projected to meet a fox. He lives in the city of Salem, where foxes are not often seen. After projecting, he drove home. When he got out of his car, a red fox was standing in the parking lot only a few feet from him. They each stood still, gazing at one another in wonder, before the red fox ran into the woods beyond the lot. Despite the cold weather and "staying-home" time of Winter, it is important to get outside at least for a short visit to stay in touch with your natural surroundings and realize the remarkable change that is about to take place.

The purpose of the Winter Solstice rite is simple. It is to ensure that the Sun's light is strengthened and continues to bring us light and warmth. At our coven's rite, we have a chorus to sing our Yuletide songs and have Sabbat cakes enough to share with all who attend. We know that turning the wheel is always successful and that the cold nights will give way to longer Summer days. This is a time for great joy, peace, and kindness here on Earth.

The High Priestess casts the circle. She charges the gold, silver, red, green, white, and black candles.

High Priestess: *The seed within the Great Mother begins to grow and grow.*

The High Priestess lights all the candles. She lights the black candle, anointing it with Yule Oil, and says: *This candle will draw to Earth all the bounty and balance of the universe.* She lights the white candle and says: *This candle will send the God's light to the world to bring bounty, balance, and peace.* She lights the gold candle and says: *This candle will bring the light of the Sun.* She lights the silver and says: *This candle will bring the light of the Moon to this sacred space. Lord and Lady, renew the light once again.*

She lights the charcoal and places Winter Solstice Incense on the charcoal and rings a little Faery bell at the four directions North, South, East, West. She puts down the bell, picks up the peyton with her left hand, and, showing it to the North, says: *I call into my circle the element of Earth, the silver wolf.* She points to the East and says: *I call the element of Fire, the red fox.* She points to the South: *I call the element of Air, the great owl.* She points to the West: *I call the element of Water, the wise salmon.*

She returns the peyton to the altar. She places the

gold candle and candlestick in a cauldron. The gold ring is taken from the altar by the High Priest and placed on the finger of the High Priestess.

All sing:

Spin merry meet,
merry meet in good measure,
follow along as we join in a dance
sing merry meet,
merry meet in the circle.
Come on along you can join in the song,
bring back the light,
light never-ending,
through dark of night,
this call we are sending,
with all our might,
bring back the light.

Bring back the light,
our hearts are open,
on solstice night,
we are invoking,
the lord of life,
bring back the light, the light

Chorus:

Queen of the stars, Queen of the Moon,
Queen of the horns, and Queen of fire,
lord of life, seed of light,
flame that warms the coldest night,
Queen of the stars, Queen of the Moon,
Queen of the horns, and Queen of fire,
hearken to this Witch's rune,

work our will as we desire,
lord of life, seed of light,
flame that warms the coldest night,
bring to us the waxing light,
be with us on solstice night.

Bring back the light,
light is descending,
to Earth tonight,
light never-ending,
to Earth tonight,
bring back the light.

Spin merry meet, merry meet in good measure.
Earth, Water, Fire, and Air,
make this year a blessing.
The light, the light, the light, the light, the light.

Then all sing:

The golden ring is the ring of the sun,
never-ending and never undone.
The oak king gives way to the holly king's return,
his death and birth does turn and turn.
The golden ring is the ring of the sun,
never-ending and never undone.

The holly leaf does prickle and sting,
the red berry colors his brow,
the holly king's ending is now.
Green is the fire, red is the cold,
black to entwine, white to unfold,
the red berry colors his brow,
the holly king's ending is now.

The holly leaf does prickle and sting,
so is the power of the golden ring.

All chant:

Mother Earth, Father Sun, we are one,
Father Sun, Mother Earth, give life birth.
Queen of snow, Queen of Earth,
seeds of starlight bring to birth,
turn the wheel and form the ring,
the Sun returns and he is king.
Mother Earth, Father Sun, we are one.

High Priest and High Priestess hold their hands above their heads and say together: *Our home, the Earth, is adorned with green holly and fir. Red is the flame of the hearth and the cauldron flames. Winter has touched the windows of our palace, and the ice sparkles with light from our sacred space. We give thanks to the Great Goddess Queen and the Holly King. The God and Goddess renew the circle of life, passion, and love with the united essence of creation. O! holy ones, plant the seed of light within the Great Mother's womb.*

The High Priest and High Priestess, holding hands, place the High Priestess's finger with the gold ring in the chalice of spring water and say together: *Flame of life that ignites and illumines the world, warming this long and cold Yule.*

High Priest: *Queen of life, we thank you for bringing the newborn Sun.*

Together the priest and priestess hold the chalice. Each takes a sip of the charged water and then places the chalice on the altar. Both touch the new Yule log, to charge it for the coming year's fire. They raise their arms to the sky and ask aloud for great bounty to bless them, their families, friends, covens, and animals.

The High Priestess then picks up the peyton in her right hand and shows it to the North and says: *I release the element of Earth; I honor the great wolf.* She faces West and says: *I release the element of Water; I honor the wise salmon.* She faces South: *I release the element of Air; I honor the great owl.* She faces East: *I release the element of Fire; I honor the red fox.*

The Sabbat cakes are then charged and passed to all who attend. The High Priestess releases the circle, and merriment abounds. The priest and priestess place last year's Yule log on the fireplace. If you don't have a fireplace, ask a friend to burn the log somewhere safely outside.

Magical Herbs

Yuletide herbs can make a holiday home a wonderfully vibrant and atmospheric place, adding beauty and dimension to the meaning of Winter Solstice. Sun plants, like mistletoe, balsam, and fir, and also any dried herbs from Summer, are predominant around this time of year, because they contain light and warmth. On Yule, when Witches decorate their homes, they do so from the doorway inward, thus inviting the light inside. We adorn doorways and mantels with evergreen boughs, bunches of dried Summer herbs, and Witch's cords in reds, blacks, greens, and golds. Our ancient ancestors brought an evergreen tree inside to mystically ensure that there would be light all year round. The evergreen retains sunlight, staying green all year, and reminds us that life is forever present and renewable.

I usually go with a few Witch friends to a tree farm to

cut down a tree, mainly because I know that the tree was grown there for that particular purpose. When we cut the tree, we perform a ritual. We thank the tree, leave a gift to the tree, either some herbs or food for the animals and birds, and start a seedling for a new tree to be planted at Beltane. One year, when we drove out to the tree farm, it was a frosty, icy day with much snow on the ground from a previous storm. The tree farm is on preserved land, near a reservoir, and is a place of great natural beauty. While we were busy with our ritual, a buck with huge antlers came out of the woods to watch us. It was Hearne, the Great Stag, welcoming the Witches and apparently making sure we were doing our job properly. He only watched for a moment or two before dashing away into the woods. Once the tree was cut, we picked it up and the smallest rabbit I ever saw—all fluffy in his Winter coat—hopped out from under the tree and bounded off in the same direction as the Stag. We were so fortunate to be a part of such a magical moment.

Mistletoe, which curls its way around the mighty oak, is sacred to the Celts and must always be cut with a golden (really bronze or brass) sickle. This heal-all herb, whose roots and leaves are used in a variety of medicinal and magical treatments, brings with it a sense of warmth, nurturing, and love. Never eat the berries; but legend says that when the greens are ingested, it brings down the blood pressure. Hanging it from your rooftop or eaves protects your home from lightning. The practice of kissing under the mistletoe is an ancient Witch tradition to ensure the spark of light between male and female. The mistletoe is an enhancement of love and romance and a symbol of fertility.

Following is a list of some of the more common Yuletide herbs, plants, flowers, and seeds:

- holly
- mistletoe
- pinecones
- pine needles
- oak leaves
- Yule log ashes
- fir
- birch
- hazel bark
- sandalwood
- ivy
- comfrey
- elder
- cinnamon
- cloves
- nutmeg
- chamomile
- sunflower
- frankincense
- myrrh
- wintergreen
- apple leaf
- dried apple

Philtres, Incense, and Oils

At the moment of Winter Solstice, past, present, and future are beautifully layered, impinging one upon the other. This exquisite moment of connection, both Earthly and Otherworldly, is reflected in the blending of a philtre, incense, or oil. The charged auras of Yuletide ingredients form a vital and timeless partnership ablaze with an inner fire released by the warmth and light of the ingredients within. Mixed in a magical bag that has been charged in a Magic Circle, the philtre can be carried on your person, hung on a Yule Witch's cord from above a doorway or window, or set out in a special bowl on a table or shelf as an aromatic, enchantment with a magical intention. Incense and oils can be burned or used in holiday spells. Herbal blends make great Yuletide gifts as well. Following are a few examples given as a starting point. These can be expanded or built upon to suit your purpose and personality. Remember, all ingredients must be charged in a sacred space before blending:

BRAN'S YULETIDE PHILTRE

crushed holly berries
dried mistletoe
gold
comfrey
elder
balsam
fir
pine needles
cinnamon
apple leaves or wood

Mix together in a special bowl for mixing philtres and place in a red magic bag. Use frankincense, myrrh, sandalwood, or orrisroot as possible fixatives to retain scent. The gold can be a piece of jewelry—a ring, perhaps, or an earring.

WINTER SOLSTICE INCENSE

pine needles
cinnamon
frankincense
myrrh
dried apple leaf or wood

Blend all ingredients. You want to make enough to use during your ritual and to share with others. Put some in a small bottle with a cork and tie a ribbon around its neck to give as a gift. To charge it, place it in a bowl in your magic space before using it in ritual.

YULE OIL

1 dram pine oil
1 dram fir oil
5 drams almond oil
1 cinnamon stick
handful of cloves
1 drop musk oil
tiny pieces of apple wood

Using almond oil as a base, blend all ingredients in an enamel pan and warm on very low heat. Let cool and place in a small bottle with a lid or cork. Musk oil can be purchased at any Witch supply store.

LOVE OIL

1 dram jasmine oil
½ dram orange oil
½ dram apple oil
5 coriander seeds
5 dried rose petals

Blend in an enamel pan on very low heat. Let cool and place in a small bottle with lid.

Magical Stones

In Winter the dark woods are lit with glistening snowfall, which dresses the land as if with jewels on every tree. Sparkling silver and white lights tell gleaming tales of wonderlands as we stand blue-lipped and chilled at the turning point of the Sun. Stones, gems, and crystals become our special companions on Yule, gifting us with both physical and spiritual meaning. Crystals and gems allow us to see in a new light many times over. They can be used to heal, or to bring us love, protection, or prosperity. As generators of light and electricity, stones help to bring us into balance with the energy and light of the land. As Witches have known for centuries, though scientists have only recently discovered, earth—actual soil—respires, taking in oxygen, breathing. Stones, though seemingly inanimate objects, are our living, energized, magical tools that leap and pulse with life.

Following is a list of magical stones to help empower our magic during the Yuletide season:

- clear quartz
- ruby
- garnet
- green tourmaline
- citrine
- jet
- diamond
- alexandrite
- kunzite

Winter Solstice Spells

When we understand our relationship to the world around us, we understand the teachings of the Goddesses and Gods and are returned to a place of peace and integration with our planet, Mother Earth. Spells help us to bring our body and mind into harmony. Often at Yule we are filled with a restlessness and an eagerness that is both exciting and a bit unsettling. Everything appears open to new interpretation. After the silence of a new-fallen snow, the glow of space seems to unfold endlessly, the resulting perspective breathtaking. Yuletide spells strive to raise your spirits and give a sense of balance, beauty, and peace.

The entire Season of Light provides us with an opportunity to reflect on the idea that pleasure is something we find outside of ourselves, but happiness is found within. The answers we seek have to include the possibility of a reality not physically perceived.

During the Winter Solstice season, I often take a nighttime walk outside to enjoy the new-fallen snow or the crisp, cool winter air. It feels good to lie down and roll in the snow or sit down on the cold ground for a minute or two to reflect upon this special time of year. When I was a little girl, my mother would bring a bowl of snow into the house. She would sweeten it with cream, sugar, and vanilla, and we'd sit in front of the fireplace to eat it. My cats would sit and wait for me to put the bowl down so they could lick it. Those were magical moments we shared, which I'll never forget. It's sad to think that my grandson cannot enjoy such a feast, because today we often cannot eat snow or drink the rainwater. Winter Solstice is a time to focus our magic on returning both ourselves and our planet to its natural balance.

Here are some meditations you can do to help connect you to your natural Winter environment, followed by a Winter Love Spell to help fend off the Winter blues.

EPONA MEDITATION

Epona is a Great Goddess of the Land who assumes the shape of a swift white horse. She roams great spiritual distances and helps to empower our magic. This meditation will help not only in the cold months but possibly later on in the year, leading you out of the Winter and into a feeling of Spring.

Find a comfortable place in which to lie down. Count into alpha. On the screen of your mind, see an ancient countryside of your ancestors. Envision a cold season, picture a steel-gray sky, and see the soft snow beginning to fall to the ground silently. Far off on a hill, a white horse appears. It is Epona the Goddess. She has made her presence known to you. Call her to you. In your mind, speak her name, Epona, Epona, and watch her as she gallops toward you. See yourself mounting her back. Hold her white glistening mane in your hands. Ask her to take you with her on a ride to the future, to show you things you need to know about your life and what lies ahead. As you ride with her, feel the soft snow on your face and arms. Take great care to tell yourself that you will remember all the things you see and hear on your ride to the future. Once the ride is over, she will take you back to where you are now. Visualize yourself getting off her back, then wave good-bye to her and thank her. Say: *I thank you, Epona, Great Goddess, I shall remember all you have shown me. I will try to embrace the correct things to come and avoid the incorrect things in my future.* Count up from alpha and immediately write down in a book or notepad all you remember.

WINTER BALANCING MEDITATION

This meditation is for balancing your nature, spirit, and physical life and will help you to see and feel your relationship to your God totem of Winter. It is important for us to see how our worldly needs connect with the needs of Mother Earth. We need warmth, fire, and sun, as well as the cleansing cold. We are so protected by our modern technology, we forget that Nature can often supply us with all we need if we are aware.

Sit in a comfortable place, but sit where you can see the cold outdoors from behind a warm window. Shut off all phones, and stay as quiet as you can for a few minutes before starting the meditation. Count into alpha. Envision the Tor, a sacred spiraling hill of magical importance in Glastonbury, England. See the rolling hills and ancient force of Nature that existed in old times. See a clear winter sky with white and gray clouds moving over the sacred hill. Soft, sugarlike snow falls gently all over you. Feel yourself walking up the spiral trail toward the top of the Tor. While you walk, the snowflakes settle on your face, your lashes, and the rim of your hooded cloak. Ahead of you the Stag, Hearne, the totem Horned God of Winter, waits at the top of the great hill. Standing majestically, he watches your steps. As you reach the top of this magical place, all you must do is reach out and touch the great Stag. You can see in your mind's eye his warm breath frozen in the air. His strong brown eyes look into yours. Reach your arms around his neck and rest your head against him. Step back and thank him for his strength and love. Bid him farewell and watch him as he bounds away to the bottom of the hill and into the ancient woods.

Look all around you, stretching out your arms, almost spinning to survey the cold countryside. Far off in the horizon you can see smoke rising from a warm hearth. It is your home. The rising smoke calls you home as the daylight dwindles. You begin your descent from the sacred hill. Down you walk, almost running into the same woods that harbors the Great Stag. As you walk toward your castle, you again see the smoke and warm glow of a welcoming hearth. Walk into the great hall. The snow melts from your clothing, hands, and face. You are greeted by the red golden glow of the flames. Step to the fireplace and warm your hands and heart. Now come back to the place where you started—in your own chair in your home—and be thankful. Count out of alpha, sip a warm cup of tea, and remember the Stag and his touch.

ALONE WITH WINTER MEDITATION

Go into alpha. Visualize yourself in the ancient woods of your ancestors at the Winter Solstice. You are naked and standing in the cold ice and snow, surrounded by barren trees and the green flora of Winter. Next to you is a rabbit with its Winter fur. A wolf and his partner stride by you. The Stag and Doe graze by you. You begin to feel the cold ground and icy breeze. What are you to do to keep the heat of your body and draw the warmth of the waning Sun to save you? Look around the forest as you search for a place of warmth and shelter. Under a tree there is a hole dug into the ground with dried fir needles all around it. It gives you an idea to find a tree that is hollowed out. You find one and stand inside awhile, but you are still cold. You begin to search for a rock or cave or natural incline that can shelter you. You begin to gather fir needles and boughs of evergreen. You pile them high and deep and begin to burrow into them, but in your shelter you begin to wail like a lost puppy. Out of the forest comes the Hare covered in fur. She sits next to you at your feet. Then come two wolves, a male and female. They come to you, kissing your face with their wet, rough tongues, and lie down one on either side of you. The Stag and Doe join in the comforting celebration and curl up together in your sheltered nest. Your body begins to warm. As the night goes by, the temperature rises and a thunderstorm appears. A bolt of lightning strikes a fallen oak branch and lights it on fire. You run and gather more wood to burn and surround the fire with stones, making a circle around it. While you tend the winter fire, stirring it and keeping it going, you pick up pieces of soft bark and feathers and begin to weave bits of shredded fur. You tie them together with strips of bark and wood, designing a cloak to wear. You have become the keeper of the flame, and the animals of the forest come to warm themselves, knowing that this is your place in Nature. The God and Goddess thank you for tending their fire and you in turn thank them for granting light and warmth in Winter.

WINTER LOVE SPELL

Winter can be a lonely season. Sometimes, in desperation, we might say things that are filled with drama and emotion. We cry out for love. It is fine and sometimes healthy to get feelings and thoughts that are bottled up out of your system, but it is also important to neutralize them so they don't bring harm to you or others. In the following spell we yearn to be loved, but we also ask that this is for the good of all. You will need:

1 pinch wolf's hair
1 quartz crystal
1 red, 1 white, and 1 black candle
1 magic wand
1 peyton
a few sprigs of mistletoe and evergreen, and a twig of holly
1 white porcelain bowl
1 red magic bag
1 green magic bag
3 silver paper stars
1 silver paper moon
Winter Solstice Incense (see p. 62)
1 thurible and instant-light charcoal
Bran's Yuletide Philtre (see p. 62)
Yule Oil (see p. 62)
Love Oil (see p. 63)
1 piece of parchment paper, 6 inches square
matches

The night before the full moon before Solstice, set your altar facing East. Put the black and red candles on the left side of the thurible and the white one on the right side. Place a few sprigs of holly, evergreen, and some wolf's hair around the white porcelain bowl. Fill the bowl with fresh snow or ice from your freezer. Place the stars and moon on the left side of the altar. Place the peyton in front of you and the two oils to the right of you. Light your charcoal. Wear a red, black, or white robe or dress. Take off your shoes and socks to feel the cool floor or ground. Cast your circle deosil, or clockwise, with your magic wand, saying:

Circle white, circle perfect, show your light, through this cold and winter night. Cast a second circle and say: *Circle red, circle perfect, show your light, perfect ring of power and light.* Cast a third circle and say: *Circle black, circle perfect, show your light, draw to me my heart's delight.*

Anoint your candles with Winter Solstice Oil and Love Oil. Sprinkle incense on the charcoal and write these words on your parchment:

"The moon shadows the hawk as it flies over the snow-covered hills. The bright moon lights the silver fur of the wolf, and the night wind carries his wail. Could my screaming heart be heard so clearly! Shall the moon's light strike my likeness into your mind, love, and heart. You are my life! my last reason for living. I ask the Gods and Goddesses that what I ask is to their liking and correct for all. I neutralize anything that is harmful. So mote it be."

HOLIDAY FARE

At the Yuletide holiday meal, food and thankfulness for the Goddess Epona's abundance takes center stage. Epona, a Goddess I often honor at Yule, has many associations with the royal symbols of horses, as do her British and Welsh counterparts, Rhiannon and Cerridwen. A mystical and intricate blending of culinary herbs provides a rich tapestry of aromas and mouthwatering flavors to delight the senses. As on every Sabbat, at Yule Witches become mistresses and masters of entertaining. Table and dining area are set in Faery splendor. Amid magical crystals and candlelight, we discover new pleasures and the bountiful satisfaction that comes from the Feast of Epona's magical gifts. Epona, the goddess who turns into a horse, rides all the realms overlooking the bounty of all. Roast turkey, winter squash, cakes, and cookies fill us with good feelings and friendly thoughts. Steaming Yuletide wassail beckons us inside, pushing back the night and warming our spirits, bodies, and minds. There is no better way to savor the spirit of the season than by sharing your home and Nature's gifts with cherished family and friends. Yuletide meals are magical, savory moments that will make a lasting impression on all who take part.

Following are some suggestions of what to serve at Yule. Keep in mind when preparing recipes that dried herbs are used in slightly smaller amounts than fresh. Of course, all herbs should be charged in a sacred space before cooking.

The Feast of Epona

Pagan Wassail
Magical Celtic Fruit Cake
Roast Turkey with Herb Stuffing
Winter Squash
Scottish Stovies
Candy Kelly's Yule Sabbat Cookies

PAGAN WASSAIL

FOR THE WASSAIL'S BAKED APPLES:

1 doz. apples
1 cup brown sugar
3 tbs. cinnamon
butter or margarine
¾ cup boiling water
2 tbs. sugar

Core apples and place in an 8 × 8-inch baking pan. Mix sugar and cinnamon, fill apples with mixture, dot tops with butter. Add boiling water and sugar to pan and bake at 375° F for 40 to 60 minutes.

FOR THE WASSAIL:

1 cup water
4 cups sugar
1 tbs. nutmeg, grated (for luck)
½ tsp. mace
2 tsp. ginger (to prevent arguments)
6 whole cloves (to influence people in high places, and for luck)
1 stick cinnamon (same)
6 whole allspice
1 doz. eggs, separated
4 bottles sherry
2 cups brandy

Combine first 8 ingredients in a saucepan and boil for 5 minutes. Beat egg whites until stiff. In a separate bowl, beat egg yolks. Fold whites into yolks. Strain spice mixture into egg mixture and stir. Combine sherry and brandy and bring almost to a boil. Gradually add liquor to spice and egg mixture, stirring rapidly as you do so. Before serving, add baked apples to foaming liquid. Serve in a large cauldron.

MAGICAL CELTIC FRUIT CAKE

8 oz. flour
1 tsp. baking powder
6 oz. currants
6 oz. sultanas
2 oz. candied or glazed cherries
2 oz. mixed fruit peel
grated lemon peel
5 oz. butter
5 oz. sugar
3 large eggs

2 tbs. finely ground almonds
sliced almonds

Line a round 7-inch cake pan with greased wax paper. Combine and sift the flour and baking powder and set aside. Mix fruit and peel and set aside. In a separate bowl cream butter and sugar together. Beat in eggs and add flour mixture slowly. Mix in ground almonds and fruit mixture and turn into cake pan. With a tablespoon, make a slight dip in the center of the fruit cake. Bake at 325° F for 2½ hours. After a half hour of baking, sprinkle top with sliced almonds.

ROAST TURKEY WITH HERB STUFFING

10–16-lb. turkey
2 lemons

Place turkey breast side up on a greased rack in roasting pan. Squeeze juice of 2 lemons inside and outside turkey to tenderize it and to infuse the energy of the sun. Preheat oven to 450° F. Roast at 350° F, basting frequently with pan drippings. Allow about 20 minutes per pound.

FOR THE STUFFING:

2 cups mushrooms, chopped (for grounding and balancing)
2 large onions, chopped, (for purity of mind, body, and spirit)
¼ cup butter, melted, or olive oil
6 cups cubed day-old white or whole wheat bread
1 cup finely chopped celery
1 tsp. tarragon or basil
¼ tsp. nutmeg

1 tsp. powdered sage
pinch thyme
¼ tsp. sea salt
freshly ground black pepper
2–4 apples, chopped fine (optional)
1–2 eggs, beaten
2 cups chicken broth, to moisten

Sauté mushrooms and onions in butter or olive oil until golden brown. Combine with bread, celery, and spices. Add apples, if desired. Add eggs. Soften with chicken broth. Stuff turkey just before cooking, leaving space for mixture to swell.

WINTER SQUASH

Winter squash is the color of the Sun—yellow or yellow orange—and a perfect dish to serve at Solstice festivities. Combined with cinnamon and ginger, herbs ruled by the Sun, the dish is infused with warm and positive magical energy.

3 or 4 winter squash, approx. 3 lbs. each
3 tbs. butter or margarine
3 tsp. brown sugar
¾ tsp. salt
½ tsp. ginger
½ tsp. cinnamon
heavy cream to taste, warmed
raisins, nuts, parsley (optional)

Peel, quarter, and boil squash until tender. Mash or beat well with an electric mixer. Add butter, sugar, salt, ginger, and cinnamon, and heavy cream until at preferred consistency. Garnish with raisins, nuts, or parsley, if desired.

SCOTTISH STOVIES

½ oz. pan drippings from meat
¼ lb. onions, sliced thin
1 lb. potatoes, sliced thick
salt and pepper
½ cup water

In a deep cast-iron skillet, melt pan drippings. Fry onions lightly and add potatoes. Season with salt and pepper to taste. Add water. Bring to a boil and simmer for 1 hour, stirring occasionally. Serve hot.

CANDY KELLY'S YULE SABBAT COOKIES

These can also be used at the Solstice ritual in addition to the sabbat cakes we made at Samhain. While making these cookies, light red and green candles and anoint with Yule Oil (see p. 62).

1 cup shortening (butter or margarine)
1 cup sugar
1 egg
1 cup warmed molasses
⅓ cup hot water
1 cup enriched white flour
1 tsp. baking soda
1 tsp. salt
1 tsp. ginger
3 tsp. cloves
3 tsp. cinnamon
3–4 cups enriched white flour

Cream shortening and sugar together. Add egg. Beat well. Add molasses and water, and stir again. Add 1 cup flour, baking soda, salt, and spices. Add rest of flour until dough is not too sticky. Chill overnight. If wrapped in wax paper, dough should keep a couple of days. Roll dough out to 1/4 inch thickness in sections on floured board. Cut out cookies into crescent shapes or stars. Bake at 350° F for 8 minutes or until edges are golden brown. (Optional: Cut cookies in circles and stars, placing stars on top of circles with an egg wash. Bake these at 350° F for 13 minutes.)

ANCIENT ACTIVITIES

Yule, with all of its pagan customs of lighting trees and displaying holly, ivy, and pine boughs in the home, shares an intimate relationship not only with Christmas but with the entire Season of Light—Chanukah, Kwanzaa, La Posadas, and St. Lucia's Day, among others. Society often overlooks the overwhelming contribution by Witches to this time of year. Christians bring trees into their homes, light candles, and give each other gifts, never really knowing why they follow such accepted social behavior. The symbolic, spiritual, cultural, religious, and ecological meaning behind our modern holiday activities is directly linked to our ancient pagan origins. Most people carry treasured, memorable moments about Yule from childhood into adulthood. As we busy ourselves with holiday preparations, do we ever ask ourselves why it is that we look forward to this magical season? Try to imagine a time when the people's nights were dark and all-encompassing. Winter is such a barren time. And though in our own age we daily reap the benefits of electricity and elaborate heating systems, we still need and yearn for warmth. Yule is the Celtic bonfires of old driven indoors by the cold weather.

The connection between Yule and today's modern holiday practices is so strong that these ancient traditions work well with holiday habits we are accustomed to. Father Winter is an ancient pagan figure whom many will recognize. He dons fur-trimmed red robes, has a white beard, and gives gifts to children. In olden times he gave fruit and plants and magical herbs. Today our community makes or buys gifts for Father Winter to give to the children. Witches burn an oak Yule log, charging another in our Magic Circle, which will be kept in a sacred space until the next Winter. This gives a place of prominence for the mighty oak, while ensuring fuel in case of an emergency. The Celts also hung small glass bowls with candles inside on their Yule trees. These we call Faery lights, their luminous arcs exquisite reminders that there are no straight lines in Nature, only the esoteric beauty of the curve. I have bought and been given many of these green hand-blown glass lights from Wales. Though I personally am concerned about a fire hazard, the Welsh still use them, and sell the candles that go with them to hang on trees. Faery lights are said to please the Faeries and attract them. Each light on the tree is said to represent the beating of a Faery's heart.

No matter how we choose to celebrate, the pagan spirit enhances and enriches the Yuletide season. Following are a few pagan activities served up with some bewitching flair:

YULE LOG CANDELABRA

The oak Yule log is the symbol of the newborn Sun. In addition to the log we keep in a sacred space until the following Yule, we sometimes make a candelabra from another oak log. Using a drill bit slightly smaller than the candles you intend to use, drill holes into the log about two inches apart. Set on a stand nestled in boughs of evergreen.

You can dress this up with pinecones and red ribbons and can also put it outside if the wind isn't blowing too hard.

Holiday Wreath

The wreath is a symbol not only of the Wheel of the Year but also of the circle of life and wisdom of the all. Its origins are pagan. Making a wreath encourages your artistry and nurtures I-did-it-myself pride, which we often need around this time of year. On a wire base or base of entwined branches, secure boughs of fir, pine, holly, or any evergreen of your choice. Decorate the wreath as simply or as elaborately as you wish. Attach ribbons of red, silver, or gold. I have often tied a ribbon to make a five-pointed star in the center of my wreath, making the wreath into a Witch's pentacle. Add cutouts of crescent-shaped moons, stars, and the Sun, magic bags of holiday herbs, or sprigs of red holly berries, pinecones, and wintergreen. The wreath should be an expression of many things: your personality, holiday spells, and desires such as protection, health, and spiritual growth.

Solstice Sugarplum Dreams Pillow

Often around Yule the air is so filled with electricity and anticipation that many of us find it difficult to sleep. Sweet dreams are the sugarplums of life. In our dreams we ask the God and Goddess to grant us wishes, and we wonder about what Father Winter is going to give us for gifts. It is important to dream of good things. Sometimes we dream of material things and sometimes of spiritual growth and peace.

Sometimes we wish for a new baby or for a new love. All of your magical intentions should be put into your dream-pillow blend. The following mixture uses sleep-enhancing magical herbs that can be placed on your nightstand in a special bowl or sewn into a magic bag and put inside your pillow.

mugwort	tiny pinch pine needles
hops	tiny pinch cinnamon
chamomile	tiny pinch rosebuds
catnip	

Using mugwort as the base, add only small amounts of the other herbs so that the scent is not too strong. Use red and green cotton batting to wrap the blend or place all ingredients in a red or green magic bag. Open your pillow and put the magic bag or batting deep inside your pillow so you won't feel it, then sew it back up. Take your pillow into a sacred space to charge it for correct dreams.

Faery Magic

Faeries come to us on Yule in peace and friendship, their voices filled with dreams and auguries fostered by ancient recollections. The silver branch is a vivid winter image, a Faery wand bearing light and sound with the powers of the *sidhe* in its seven bells. To make a silver branch wand, see p. 17. You can also wear silver bells or hang them from a special tree or branch, which then can become a silver branch wand. Witches understand the inseparable nature of light and sound. As light travels, it vibrates. As forces vibrate, they give off light. Bells are messages of light and sound sent to us by the Faeries. On Yule, bells ring soft and clear seemingly with the power to soothe an aching heart or bend the knotted oak. In the aftermath of celebration, the music of bells brings an uncomplicated happiness. By honoring the Winter Solstice, another link has been forged in the new chain that carries us to the next turn of the Wheel. We look to the future for trust and confidence. We look to the Faeries to help us find the future. All Winter we wait for the Faery charms—at Yule they come at last.

THE CRYSTAL WISH GAME

Here is a game we often play during the Yuletide ritual. Each participant is given a wrapped crystal. Some are beautiful cut crystals and some little more than dirt! Every time the silver branch rings, you give whatever package you have to the next person. In other words, you never know if you are getting the troll or the Faery crystal. Each time you exchange packages you have to make a wish. If you give yours away begrudgingly, your wish probably won't come true. If you give it away with a good heart, then your wish probably will come true. But the point of the game is that it doesn't matter if your wish comes true or not. It's the art of giving that brings you good things!

It is always fun and interesting to see how people react to this game, which was designed by the Faeries to teach us how to give. Our instincts are to hold on to what we've got. When the bell rings, many people don't want to give the crystal away. One year there was a beautiful amethyst in the bunch. I could see the pained looks on people's faces when they got the rock instead of the gem. Sometimes people are so materialistic that they can't accept something less than perfect, even in a tiny little crystal. The game can bring to light a person's sense of greed, or lack of a sense of giving.

Sometimes it helps to meditate on why you got what you got or just about giving in general. What the Faeries tell us with the game is that the rock, whether gem or stone, is from the Earth and a gift with meaning only you can discern. After the ritual the game continues with the host or hostess ringing the silver branch at random times throughout the Yuletide meal signaling all to swap.

IMBOLC
(February 1st)

★

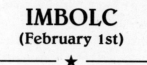

There is a youngness and Springtime glory about the festival of Imbolc, which at first appears to be out of step with February's stark and bitter Winter face. In the silence of February mornings, we still wake to rime-edged windowpanes and air so pure and thin it cuts like crystal through the wind. We are reminded during this time of year that the icy frost lies just beyond the door, and so we make ourselves content with home and familiar things.

The Goddess continues to thrive in her Crone phase in February, but at Imbolc, Witches honor the Celtic Triple Goddess Brid (pronounced *breed)* in her maiden aspect. (She is also sometimes called Brigid, Brigit, or Bride.) As Protector and Preserver of All Memory and Knowledge, Brid shares many characteristics with Dana, the Mother of All Gods, whose origins reach back to Earth's beginnings. Brid is daughter of the Dagda, whom we met at Samhain, the "Good God" who performs perfectly at all he tries to do. Brid is foster-mother to so many vital traditions that to me she speaks also of the Celtic Lady of the Lake, whose roles are primarily those of teacher and magical instructor. Brid empowers her students with the wisdom and knowledge to nurture the land, keeping it safe and productive and for the good of all.

At every point on the Wheel of the Year, Earth's virginity in effect renews itself. At each festival we celebrate this renewal as the bringing forth of light from the Sun. On Imbolc, Brid is honored in her maiden aspect, but she is a pregnant maiden, pregnant with the young seed of the Sun. As such, Brid is Goddess of Fire and Fertility. At Imbolc, which is also called the Festival of Lights, Brid wears a radiant crown of candles. She is wondrous Healer, Protector, and Patron of Creative Inspiration. Until her light is fully born again at Beltane, Brid ensures that the seed is nurtured inside her womb and that the home fires continue to burn through the final days and nights of Winter.

Thus it is that, even with the cold hands of February still upon our shoulders, the promise of Spring is begun. Beneath the crisp, ice-encrusted soil, life is indeed starting anew. The tiny green leaves and white bell-shaped heads of strong and eager snowdrops emerge from between the rocks and snow. Certain species of birds return in anticipation of the increasing light and warmth from the Sun, and Spring constellations can sometimes be seen in the night Sky. On Imbolc, Witches prepare grains to be planted at Beltane in May, which we have saved from the previous Summer and Autumn harvests. I often begin seedlings now that will green and color my garden in Springtime.

Winter is nearing an end, and as we cast off the darkness, we, too, begin to feel and flirt with a flourishing or blossoming from within. We hear Earth's hidden voices and, bound as we are to the rhythms of the universe, we listen for voices hidden deep inside ourselves. Brid is guardian not only of the physical flame but of the spark of spirituality as well. As the Mother to All Memory and Preserver of All Knowledge, she brings intelligence and wisdom to our unwrought spiritual yearnings. Around this time of year I often reflect upon the strength and promise of joy that Brid is offering me. I am thankful for the growing light and warmth from the Sun and am reminded of my responsibilities both to myself and to those in my community. Often during the Imbolc season, Witches bring food and warm blankets to local soup kitchens and shelters. Imbolc is a time to give and share with others, as Brid gives and shares her enchanted and empowering Light.

WHICH WITCH IS WHICH? CLARIFYING THE ORIGINS OF THE WORD

Perhaps no other word in the English language has been perverted as blatantly as the word *Witch.* Its definition has evolved over many centuries. The Anglo-Saxon *wicca* or *wicce* simply refers to a male or female seer or person who can find out information by using magic. *Wych* in Saxon and *wicce* in Old English meant "to bend, turn, or shape." The earlier Indo-European root word *wic* or *weik* meant the same thing. The Germanic root *wit* means "to know." There are no other known original meanings of the word. Religionists, anthropologists, and sociologists are to blame for the umbrella use of the word *Witch.* This word does not describe magic used in any culture other than the Celtic tribes, and therefore has been used inaccurately throughout academia for hundreds of years. The word simply does not exist in any other culture. When people refer to voodoo or satanism as forms of Witchcraft, they are misusing the word and in such a derogatory manner that it ultimately harms others.

Richard A. Horsley, Associate Professor of Religion at the University of Massachusetts, Boston, discusses in his excellent article, "Who Were the Witches?" in the *Journal of Interdisciplinary History,* IX, 4 (Spring, 1979), how the decisions made in the sixteenth and seventeenth century European witch trials were all based on church, or canon, law. Church law defined the word *witch* inaccurately, to say the least, and not according to the original Celtic pagan meaning offered above. It was not until the judicial system developed the philosophy that decisions had to be made based on fact and not on mythical or church interpretations that the word *witch* could even begin to live down the horrific connotations attached to its original meaning.

Long before the sixteenth century, as hostile patrifocal societies grew up around the matrilineal societies of the Celtic tribes, the Celtic people were forced into organized warfare. With the growth of Christianity, the Celtic culture and language suffered an horrific fate and, in many instances, irreversible damage. The word *witch* was perverted to mean something completely foreign to its original root form. It is particularly disturbing to me when the media or individuals equate Witchcraft with satanism or the devil. There is no devil or Satan in our religion. Christianity brought their Satan with them while invading Celtic lands. The Celts never divided things into black and white, good and evil. To do so would be against Nature. Nature is complex, and people possess a variety of characteristics and nuances of emotions and thoughts. Witchcraft has nothing to do with satanism. The word *witch* has never been proven to mean anything more than "magic maker." Indeed, if a Witch were close to anything in Christianity, it would be an angel, not a devil!

EARTH MAGIC

The significance and scope of Brid's powers cannot be emphasized enough during Imbolc. The word *imbolc* literally translates as "in milk." In ancient times, milk from sheep was crucial to a tribe's survival of Winter. Ewes must become pregnant and give birth before they are able to lactate and produce milk. As Goddess of Fertility, Brid presides over the birth of newborn lambs, which occurs at this time of year.

In ritual, we pour milk or cream into the Earth, thanking her, nurturing her, and thus returning the fertility and bounty She so generously gives to us. As partners and sharers in the universe, Witches have embraced the idea for centuries—only recently taken up by environmentalists and conservationists—that life here on Earth is an intensely reciprocal arrangement. As William Wordsworth once wrote (apparently inspired by the Poet Goddess Brid!): "Nature never did betray the heart that loved her." We must end the insensitive and injurious practice of taking from our planet without ever giving back. If you cut down a tree, thank it, and plant another in its place. If you harvest the land, replenish the soil. These are ideas that come from the common sense of natural law and the simple magic of the universe.

The Imbolc ritual symbolizes the importance of sharing and community and the growing hope that I personally believe exists for this world and the next. Although we have been running and trying to hide from her messages for some time now, the Goddess will never allow us to fully shirk our responsibility to her. I also do not believe that it is one of humanity's desires or aims to live for too much longer in a world with undrinkable water, unbreathable air, and unplantable soil. We share an inseparable relationship with the Goddess; it is impossible to break or sever, no matter how hard society so foolishly tries. The festival of Imbolc pays homage to that bond and to the ideal balance Mother Earth is eternally offering her children.

Preparations

Because we are honoring the return of Brid in her maiden aspect, white, the color of the maiden, is the predominant hue of the Imbolc altar. White candles abound at Imbolc, and you should bring in as many as will fit on your altar and in your sacred space. The Sun is waxing and the days are growing longer. Candlelight emphasizes this season of growing light and warmth. The altar's cloth is white and the altar itself should be adorned with white flowers if you can find them. We also honor the entire triplicity of the Goddess at Imbolc. Brid arrives in her maiden aspect, but she appears, as do all the Goddesses, under the three auspices of Maiden, Mother, and Crone. We place a red and a black candle on the altar to symbolize the Mother and Crone, respectively. A black cast-iron cauldron represents the womb of the Goddess or the Goddess herself. The cauldron is an essential symbol for any holiday altar, but at Imbolc, when we are honoring the Goddess of Fertility, it is especially meaningful. A piece of ash, Imbolc's symbolic tree, should also be present on the altar whether in the form of a charm, staff, or magic wand.

Specifically for the ritual below you will need 3 white candles, 3 black candles, a red candle, a green candle, an ash pot, a broom, a peyton, 2 chalices filled with milk, a bowl, Brid's Philtre, Brid's Oil, Imbolc Incense (see pp. 95–6), 3 garnets, a hematite, a ritual blade, a wand, a thurible, a charcoal, altar matches, a lodestone, packets of seeds for flowers, vegetables, and trees, vervain, wolf's hair, Faery Fire Oil (see p. 96), Brid's Corn Dolly (see p. 107), and some grain, wheat, or corn.

It is always correct to bathe before you go into a magic space or perform a ritual. Here is a Lady of the Lake bath and meditation you can do to focus your energies and magic before the Imbolc ritual:

Fill your tub with warm water. Place some dried chamomile, violet, and lemon peel in a magic bag or silk or gossamer cloth, and tie it with white or aqua-colored ribbon. Throw this herbal blend into the bath. Light an aqua-colored candle and set it on the edge of the tub. Put on some relaxing Celtic music. Fill the tub quite full, then lie down in the water. Vision yourself as the Lady of the Lake. See your hair as long and flowing and your gown as white, watery green, and blue, sparkling like sunlight on water. See a delicate chain-mail gauntlet upon your right hand. Rest and relax, and image the power of the Goddess that can exist under the water as well as on land. She is both Fire and Water. She can be envisioned like a flaming candle floating along the water. Vision Excalibur, the sword of truth and courage, in your right hand. When you feel the weight and power of the sword in your grip, lift your hand high above you and say out loud:

> *Here is the power of the* sidhe. *Here in this sword is the power of Dana. I am the daughter of Dana, and the Lady of the Lake is my sister, keeper of courage.*

Then rest your arm in the water. Remain there for as long as you can continue the image and the sweet, strong feelings. After the bath, allow the candle to continue to burn. You might float it on some of your bath water after you've stepped out. Put on a white, aqua, or rose-colored robe before getting dressed for your ritual.

What to Wear

At Imbolc, we often wear white robes. You can always wear black, or for this particular holiday, green, rose, or aqua. Vestments and stoles can be adorned with symbols or runes of the Moon and Sun, a flame, sprouting seeds, and so on. You might also want to represent Brid by braiding white flowers in your hair or into a bracelet.

The Ritual

Set the altar and cast the circle. Place the broom, bristles upright, behind the door where you receive guests.

The High Priestess lights the candles and says: *The Goddess has returned from the holy land, Avalon. She is Maiden once more. I charge these candles with the power of Brid to draw into this magic place all knowledge that is needed for our sovereignty.*

The High Priest lights the charcoal and sprinkles incense on it and says: *O! holy herbs, givers of light and strength, send your gentle powers to the air. Blow the strength of Brid's spirit across the sacred world.*

The High Priest holds up the peyton to the North with his left hand: *I call the element of Earth, I ask the Aisling (Faery) to come.* He holds the peyton to the East and says: *I call the element of Fire and I ask the Aisling to come.* He points to the South and says: *I call the element of Air and I ask the Aisling to come.* He points to the West and says: *I call the element of Water and I ask the Aisling to come.* He places the peyton on the altar.

The High Priestess anoints her own wrists, forehead, and back of her neck with a touch of Brid's Oil and anoints the High Priest in the same way. She lifts one chalice filled with milk and she holds the chalice in the space between the candles over the smoke of the thurible.

High Priestess: *I call into this magical place the Great Goddess Brid. I ask that she bless this milk. We thank you, mighty Goddess.*

She places that chalice on the altar and picks up the second chalice.

The High Priest picks up the blade and lifts it to the sky, saying: *I draw to this magical place the powers of the God that grows.*

He places the blade in the second chalice filled with milk and says: *Sun and Earth combine. We drink the waters of life.*

He wipes the blade and sets it down. The High Priestess drinks some milk and hands the chalice to the priest. He in turn takes a drink. He pours the rest of this milk into the bowl on the altar and says: *The waters of life shall bring protection, health, fertility, growth, clean waters, rich earth, bountiful crops for all. So mote it be.*

The High Priestess sprinkles incense on the charcoal. Again, as the smoke rises, she asks all present to speak their spells. One by one they come to the front of the altar carrying their written spells on parchment paper. Each one says a spell out loud and then lights the parchment on fire from one red candle and places the parchment into the ash pot. The priest and priestess and all present concentrate on each spell as it is spoken. After each spell burns, everyone raises their arms to release the energy of the burning spell.

After all spells are said and done the High Priestess says: *We are the Tuatha de Danaan. We honor the Goddess Mother, Dana, and the Father God, the Dagda. Brid, daughter and Goddess, we thank you for granting us the ability to know all things and to be able to heal the Earth. This promise is sweet. I am your light on this Earth.*

She anoints the three garnets with Faery Fire Oil and she holds the three garnets in her left hand. She says: *I shall keep your light and power within my body.*

The High Priest picks up the hematite, anoints it with Faery Fire Oil, and holds it in his hand, saying: *I promise to keep your power alive to heal this Earth and protect all of nature.*

Both priest and priestess pick up packets of seeds, holding them in both hands. Together they say: *I charge these seeds with the power of Brid to grow and replenish the Earth.*

The High Priest and High Priestess place the Brid Corn Dolly on the altar and sprinkle vervain and wolf's hair around the altar. The High Priest says: *Great God and Goddess, grant us protection.*

The High Priest and High Priestess reach their hands to the sky, and all who attend follow, releasing the cone of power. All kneel down and touch the ground with both hands. All rise.

The High Priestess takes her wand, and the High Priest picks up the peyton in his right hand, showing it to the North, and says: *I release the element of the Earth. I bid the Aisling farewell and to please return again.* He points to the West: *I release the element of Water. I bid the Aisling farewell and to please return again.* He points to the South and says: *I release the element of Air. I bid the Aisling farewell and to please return again.* He points to the East: *I release the element of Fire. I bid the Aisling farewell and to please return again.*

Then the High Priestess releases the circle with her wand. The milk left over in the bowl is taken outdoors to a sacred space or someplace where there is ground and is poured into the Earth. The Brid Corn Dolly is hung in either the High Priestess's or the High Priest's home.

Magical Herbs

Brid is harbinger of the healing Spring. February can be a wearying time of colds and sore throats, among many other bothersome ailments. Brid's light helps to restore our strength and resolve, while her fire serves to purify and cleanse. At this time of year we use herbs, seeds, dried fruits, and plants in Spring tonics and potions. Imbolc herbs and ingredients are charged with the energy of the Sun as well as purifying elements that will help bring clarity and well-being to the body and the spirit. A common February brew made from lemon, garlic, and honey will both warm and heal you. If you are not partial to the flavor of garlic, try just the lemon and honey with a tiny pinch of sage. If even a pinch of sage turns up your nose, try getting your hands on some heather honey. The Scots make the best I've ever sampled, but the recipe, I'm sure, was a gift from the Goddesses. Heather honey is Otherworldly delicious!

Chamomile and rose hip tea are popular Winter drinks that are powerful sources of vitamin C. Witches often harvest and save rose hips from their rose bushes at Lughnasadh in August to eat and drink all Winter long. In the former Soviet Union, where Winter can be particularly barren and citrus fruits difficult to obtain, farmers were required to devote a certain amount of acreage and labor to the production of rose hips. The sunflower is another healing, life-sustaining plant often used during Imbolc. All but the stalk of a sunflower—leaves, potatolike root, seeds, and yellow flower—can be ingested to bring the healing light of the Sun inside.

The herbs of Imbolc play both a practical and a spiritual role, in some cases fortifying your strength and endurance, and in others making you feel good about yourself emotionally and spiritually. Following is a list of some of the more essential ones Witches often use around this time of year:

- heather
- dried sage
- celandine
- lemon
- honey
- dried chamomile
- coriander seeds
- garlic
- rose hips
- ash leaf or wood
- witch hazel or hazel leaves
- sunflower seeds
- dried sunflower petals
- vervain
- violets
- wheat
- corn
- grains
- myrrh
- storax
- balsams
- dragon's blood
- benzoin
- mastic

Philtres, Incense, and Oils

Many of the ingredients on the above list are not meant to be ingested, but used to heal and cleanse in a magical philtre, incense, or oil. Chamomile, myrrh, and heather (if you can find heather at this time of year) are wonderful to burn as incense. To help bring back the light of the Sun, blend dried sage and celandine in a cup and toss the herbs onto a fire. Burning incense sends the spirit of light and smoke into the universe, purifying and cleansing the air.

Imbolc's symbolic tree, the ash tree, is often used in magical blends. The Celts regarded the ash to be so sacred, they would never cut it down. Today, though, if you have to cut an ash branch, it helps matters plenty if you are a Witch. Before cutting, thank the tree and ask for protection and permission from Merlin the magician/god who lives in the trees and often assumes their form. Cut the branch with a golden sickle that has been charged for this particular intent in your Magic Circle. If you don't have a sickle, you can use your ritual blade. It is much better luck, and much more in keeping with tradition, however, if you happen upon an ash branch already on the ground. Furthermore, it is considered extremely good fortune to find one on the ground that has been struck by lightning. The magical energies contained in the ash tree are said to be so potent that simply passing an ash branch over you will heal you.

Here are a few examples to get you started in creating your own Imbolc blends:

BRID'S PHILTRE

Approximately 1 teaspoon of each of the following:

heather
sage
rose hips
ash leaf
hazel leaf
chamomile
benzoin or dragon's blood

Mix all ingredients together in a bowl specifically used for making philtres. Use benzoin or dragon's blood as a fixative for retaining the aroma of the herbs.

BRID'S OIL

2 drams almond oil or olive oil
1 dram sage oil
1 dram dragon's blood
crushed garnet

Warm slowly on a very low heat in an enamel pan. Let cool and place in small corked bottles or jars. Charge the oil in your Magic Circle, wear it, or use it to anoint candles in your rituals and spells.

IMBOLC INCENSE

heather
sage
chamomile
benzoin, dragon's blood, storax, or myrrh

Blend all ingredients and keep in a magic bag, bottle, or jar.

FAERY FIRE OIL

1 garnet
1 dram dragon's blood
1 dram almond oil
coriander seeds

Warm all ingredients in an enamel pan on low heat. Allow to cool and place in a clear, white, or aqua-colored bottle.

Magical Stones

Stones, metals, and gems are gifts from the Goddess that bring messages of all kinds for us to decipher and embrace. Some stones are soft and pliable, others coarse and sharp, and still others solid, smooth, and unyielding. At Imbolc we glory in the new seed of the Sun that is gathering more and more light and strength each day. In view of such nearby promise, we sometimes become anxious about remaining healthy and warm and strong until the light is fully reborn in Spring. The stones of Imbolc help to allay these feelings of fear and uncertainty by generating the light of the Sun and by ensuring us protection against any harmful or incorrect forces.

Iron, ruled by Mars, is for protection. Imbolc is a good time of year to use iron to build a sense of security for both yourself and your home. I have huge iron spikes buried in the cornerstones of my home. Bowls of iron filings can be placed on windowsills to protect against burglaries or break-ins. An iron horseshoe has a great deal of magical power and importance. The idea of the "lucky horseshoe" began from the Witch practice of placing horseshoes with the open ends up over doors and entryways. By positioning the horseshoe up, negative energy enters one end, is neutralized in the ring, and sent packing out the other end.

Following is a list of Imbolc stones that bring messages of strength, protection, and well-being:

clear quartz
citrine
yellow tourmaline
green tourmaline
rose quartz
iron
hematite
lodestone
ruby
garnet
red zircon

Magical Spells

To the ancient Celts, February was still "staying home" time. Today we often think of it as a good month in which to get things done. Casting spells helps to define and focus our spiritual and physical desires for the future. At Imbolc, Witches project for fertility and protection in our lives. I like to meditate on the growing light from the Sun around this time of year. Because I am a Water sign, a Pisces, I have a lot of psychic energy, but I need physical strength, which the Sun gives. Attracting the Sun's warmth bolsters my energies and strengthens my health, so I can better face and enjoy the final days of the Winter season.

The signs of Earth's renewal are invigorating against February's backdrop of wintry glens and steel-gray skies. The full bloom of Spring is just around the corner. Imbolc is a good time to get your life in order. Make plans, organize, even clean your closets to bring a refreshing sense of ushering in the new and clearing away the old. Preparing your home and yourself ahead of time will allow you to take full advantage of the imminent joy and freedom of Spring.

VERVAIN AND THREE BLACK CANDLES SPELL

You will need:

3 black candles
3 brass candlesticks
3 heaping tbs. vervain

Get into your magic space. Pick up each candle and repeat out loud:

By the power of the Triple Goddess Brid, this candle will protect my home, family, friends, animals, covens, and me. So mote it be.

Pick up each candle and charge. Place the candles in their

candlesticks and put them close together. Sprinkle the vervain in three interlocking rings around each candlestick. Light the candles, and sit for a moment staring into the candle flame. Envision the Goddess Brid placing three rings of light around all that you want to protect. Then release the circle. Let the candles burn. Never blow out candles with a spell on them. Use a candle snuffer or a spoon.

CELTIC LADY OF THE LAKE COURAGE SPELL

You will need:

- *1 wand*
- *Imbolc Incense (see p. 96)*
- *Brid's Oil (see p. 96)*
- *1 black, blue, or aqua candle*
- *1 white candle*
- *1 aquamarine*
- *1 quartz crystal*
- *1 lodestone*
- *1 garnet*
- *1 chalice*
- *1 sword or picture of a sword*
- *1 small glass bottle*
- *1 charcoal and thurible*
- *1 cup spring water*
- *1 piece parchment*
- *1 green or blue pen*
- *1 aqua, blue, or green magic bag*

Cast your circle. Set the altar. Light the candles and anoint with Brid's Oil. Light the charcoal and sprinkle Imbolc Incense upon it. Raise your hands upward and say:

I call the Lady of the Lake to my sacred space and in my Magic Circle.

Pick up the sword and say:

Strike this sword with your might. Great Lady, hold my hand as I charge this chalice with your power.

Raise the sword as if you and the Lady of the Lake were lifting the sword out of the water. Touch the tip of the sword into the chalice of spring water. After you have placed the clear crystal in the water, place the sword on the altar and write this spell on the parchment with a green or blue pen:

"Lady of the Lake, grant to me (write your name) the courage to see the truth of my life and to understand the truth when it is told to me. Help me to lift the spirit sword to protect my rights and the right of all Witches, for the good of all. So mote it be."

Lift the cup and sip the holy water, sprinkle more incense, and smudge the spell in the smoke. Speak the words out loud. Keep this spell. Do not burn it. Pick up crystal, lodestone, garnet, and aquamarine, charge them, and touch them to the sword. Put stones into the magic bag to carry for courage. Keep your spell folded in your wallet or purse or keep it on your home altar. Release your circle with your wand.

BRID'S SPELL FOR ALL KNOWLEDGE

You will need:

1 black candle
1 white candle
1 red candle
1 rose quartz
1 garnet
1 clear quartz crystal
1 chalice with spring water
Brid's Oil (see p. 96)
Imbolc Incense (see p. 96)
1 wand
charcoal and thurible
1 ritual blade
1 red pen
1 red magic bag
1 piece parchment
1 ash pot

Set the altar, placing the black and red candles on the left and the white on the right. Place the thurible and ash pot in the center. Cast your circle and anoint your candles with

Brid's Oil. Sprinkle incense over the charcoal. Write on parchment with red ink the following:

"I call the power of Brid to bring to me (your name) the knowledge that I need to have a career that is successful. I ask to be granted the awareness, ability, and enthusiasm to bring my career to fruition and success. I ask that this is for the good of all. So mote it be."

Sprinkle more incense on the charcoal. Hold the parchment in the smoke and speak the words out loud to the Goddess Brid. After you've finished, touch the parchment with Brid's Oil, light the parchment in the flame of the black candle, and allow it to burn in the ash pot. When the flames die out, raise your hands to the sky and say out loud:

Thank you, Great Goddess.

Pick up the rose quartz crystal in your left hand and touch it with Brid's Oil. Place your right hand over them and say:

I charge these crystals to bring to me the knowledge of Brid.

Put down the crystals and pick up your blade. Hold it in the smoke and say:

This magic blade shall bring the energy of Brid into my chalice.

Put the blade into the water and envision her knowledge and power going into the water as the fire of Brid. Then drink the water with slow sips, feeling her energy entering your body to give you her wisdom. Place the crystals and some of the Imbolc Incense in your magic bag, hold it over the smoke, and charge it. Release your circle with your wand, keep the ashes of your spell in the bag, too, and keep the magic bag with you.

HOLIDAY FARE

Brid's light brings sustenance in many forms, but food is surely one of her more tangible and pleasurable gifts. Rich, creamy milk and egg dishes are the mainstay of Brid's Feast to symbolize the fertility and life-affirming qualities she represents. Soups, stews made from chicken, beef, or lamb, and any dish using milk or eggs are often served at an Imbolc dinner. In my coven, we usually gather together for potluck banquets or stone-soup suppers where everyone brings a dish to share with everyone else. Every Imbolc Eve, we leave food and drink outside for the Faeries, animals, and birds. The day after the feast, continuing in the Imbolc spirit of sharing and community, we often visit hospitals or bring food and supplies to those less fortunate than us.

In the following recipes, if you are concerned about the fat content of cream and milk, you can substitute low-fat milk or "light" brands of cream. Also, use organic meats and vegetables whenever possible.

THE FEAST OF BRID

Faery Wine
Wise and Creamy Salmon Soup
Asparagus Spears with Herb White Sauce
Celtic Salmon Tart
Magical Cream Puffs

FAERY WINE

1½ cups milk per serving
1 tsp. honey
⅛ tsp. vanilla extract
cinnamon

Warm milk, being careful not to boil. To each glass or mug add honey and vanilla. Sprinkle tops with cinnamon.

WISE AND CREAMY SALMON SOUP

The salmon is the wisest and most ancient of living animals. Brid is Guardian of All Knowledge and Keeper of All Memory.

1 pkg. cream cheese, cut into cubes
1 cup milk
2 tsp. dijon mustard (to bring wealth)
1½ tsp. chopped fresh dill or ½ tsp. dried dill (for protection of home and job)
2 green onions with tops sliced (for purity)
1 can chicken broth
12 oz. smoked salmon, flaked, or 1 can, drained and flaked

Heat cream cheese, milk, mustard, dill, onions, and chicken broth in a saucepan over medium heat until cheese is melted and smooth. Stir in salmon and heat until hot and ready to serve.

ASPARAGUS SPEARS WITH HERB WHITE SAUCE

Asparagus spears are for grounding; ruled by Earth and Venus. Snap ends and steam asparagus for 6 to 8 minutes, or until tender, in vegetable steamer.

FOR THE SAUCE:

2 tbs. margarine or butter
2 tbs. flour
1/4 tsp. salt
1/8 tsp. pepper
1 tsp. dill
dash sage
dash nutmeg
1 cup milk

Heat margarine over low heat until melted. Stir in flour, salt, pepper, dill, sage, and nutmeg. Cook over medium heat, stirring constantly; remove from heat when mixture is smooth. Stir in milk. Heat to boiling, stirring constantly for 1 minute. Pour sauce over spears when ready to serve.

CELTIC SALMON TART

6 oz. shortcrust pastry
2 large eggs
2 oz. grated cheese
salt and pepper
1/4 pt. cream
1/2 oz. butter
2 oz. onions
4 oz. cooked salmon

Lightly grease a round cake or pie tin and line with pastry to the rim. Beat eggs and cheese together, then add salt and pepper and cream. Melt butter in a small saucepan. Add onions and cook slowly until lightly browned. Add salmon. Cook a minute or two more, then turn contents of pan into egg mixture. Blend together and pour into pastry shell. Bake at 350° F until golden brown. Serve hot or cold.

MAGICAL CREAM PUFFS

FOR THE PUFFS:

1 cup water
½ cup butter or margarine
1¼ cups flour
4 eggs

Bring water and butter to a boil in a saucepan. Lower heat and add flour. Stir on low heat until batter forms a ball shape. Remove from the heat. Add eggs and beat until smooth. Drop, using a tablespoon, onto ungreased cookie sheet. Bake for 30 minutes until golden brown at 375° F.

FOR THE FILLING:

½ cup sugar
2 tbs. cornstarch (ruled by the Sun; brings health and wealth)
¼ tsp. salt
2 cups milk
2 egg yolks
2 tbs. butter or margarine
2 tsp. vanilla extract
confectioner's sugar

In a saucepan, slowly bring sugar, cornstarch, and salt to a boil, stirring constantly until thick. Add milk and egg yolks and boil for 1 minute. Remove from heat and add butter and vanilla. Let cool. Fill puffs with cream filling and sprinkle with confectioner's sugar.

ANCIENT ACTIVITIES

In New England, some of our heaviest snowstorms occur in February. We are often forced by the elements to stay indoors even though our hearts and minds are racing toward and yearning for Spring. February is a time of creativity and inspired imagination, as the Goddess Brid protects and guards the wellsprings of knowledge and the magical arts. With more time on our hands, we realize that the climate is right for accomplishing tasks we have left undone for too long. Checking herb closets and racks; sorting through old clothes and giving what you've outgrown to friends, relatives, or charities; clearing shelves of old paperbacks and files; and cleaning out cellars and attics are just a few of the things we often find ourselves taking on in the month of February.

Doing fun things during this month is also important, helping to pass the time, save your sanity, and hasten the arrival of Spring. During the Imbolc season there are many crafts and activities that have their roots in Celtic tradition. Grains and milk were sacred to the ancient tribes. Baking breads and making butter have changed from solemn rituals to Imbolc holiday activities. To make butter, simply put some heavy cream into a jar, close the lid, and start shaking. Making butter is a favorite activity for children and a good way to keep them entertained for a few hours or until their arms grow tired from shaking and they have to pass the jar off to the next person.

The Celts were known for their intricate knotwork and for weaving spells and magical intentions into fabric, cords, branches, or chaffs of wheat and grain. Around Imbolc, Witches often weave shapes, symbols, Celtic runes, or dollies from such material. Brid's Wheel, a Celtic symbol of energy and motion, is an intricate pattern forming the shape of Brid's Cross inside a circle. If you are interested in trying to make one, there are books devoted entirely to creating Celtic patterns by weaving and knotwork, which can be purchased at bookstores specializing in Celtic history and mythology or through Witch mail-order supply catalogs (see Sources). You can often find a Brid's Wheel, usually as a charm for a bracelet or on other jewelry, in shops specializing in Irish goods. I have a jar filled with herbs whose lid is in the shape of Brid's Wheel. The scent of the herbs comes through the opening in the center of the Wheel, which is called the Eye of the Goddess. A Brid's Wheel can also be hung on a tree or Witch's cord for magical energy and growth. Brid's Corn Dolly, however, is easy to make and a fun project to take part in on Imbolc Eve.

BRID'S CORN DOLLY

On the Wheel of the Year, Lughnasadh is Imbolc's polar opposite. Traditionally, the grain or corn from the last harvest of Lughnasadh is saved to make corn dollies at Imbolc. The corn or grain represents Brid as the Goddess of Fertility in her maiden aspect. You can make a corn dolly or representation of the Goddess Brid with a simple dried ear of corn or chaff of wheat tied with a white ribbon. If you want to dress her up, wrap her in a piece of white lace or white fabric. You can also, instead of using a white ribbon, tie a braid around the corn or grain using three ribbons or cords of Imbolc's colors—white, black, pink, or green. If you want to make a representation of the Goddess, but live in an urban area where you can't get dried corn or wheat, go to a grocery store and buy kasha or oatmeal. Charge the grain in your Magic Circle, place it in a square of silk or white fabric, and tie it together with a white ribbon. A more elaborate dolly can be made from corn husks that you bend and tie with string or ribbon to form a head, arms, and long skirt. Your Brid's Corn Dolly can be lain in a basket, called Brid's Bed, with white flowers or lace, or can be hung from doorways or eaves on your home as amulets of protection and fertility.

Faery Magic

The art of scrying, or looking into the future, began with the ancient tribes observing the flight of birds. When the birds flew in a certain direction or formation in the sky, the Celts knew that Winter would soon be arriving. The return of the birds foretold the coming of Spring. During the Imbolc season, the more birds you see and the more birds' songs you hear means the better Spring will be. Lark's song in particular is a sign of good luck and good weather. The wren is a magical bird that brings omens and sweet spells. These simple messages of the future are from the Goddess and are as viable today as they were for the ancient Celts thousands of years ago. Bird feathers also bring auguries of what will or might be. Imbolc is usually a good time to find feathers on the ground.

At Imbolc, I like to meditate on the meaning and messages of birds. Following is a bird meditation I find particularly helpful around this time of year.

IMBOLC BIRD MEDITATION

Sit quietly, close your eyes, and count into alpha. Picture a meadow with rolling hills around it. You envision small herds of sheep and cows grazing on hay and wheat and some of the sparse greens that are beginning to grow on the warm places on the hills. Feel yourself walking among the sheep and gentle cows. As you walk along, you begin to hear a bird singing. This is a magical bird bringing you good news and things you need to hear that clear your mind of worry. While listening to the bird's song you walk up to a gentle cow or ewe and ask for a handful of fresh milk to drink. Magically the milk appears in your hand. Sip the warm milk, gaze at the cool sky, then begin to walk back to where you were. As you walk, look down at your feet and notice the tiny flowers trying to bloom. Breathe the freshness of the air, and be one with the bird's song. Try to remember at least one of the bits of information you thought of during this Imbolc stroll. Count back up from alpha and immediately write down any information the bird's song gave you or the fresh new feelings you had communicating with this nature scene. Occasionally you may hear the bird's song when you need to be good to yourself or less hard on yourself.

The definition of scrying has been expanded over the ages. There are many ways to foretell the future in addition to meditations and the flight patterns of birds. Witches also use water, flame, crystals, and runes, among many other tools, in order to divine the coming year. On Imbolc Eve, as we stand on the brink of Spring, we try to look into the Otherworld to see what promise or problems might lie ahead. An Imbolc scrying box is a fun way to sample a taste of Spring in the final chilling days of Winter.

IMBOLC SCRYING BOX

Place the following items in a box and write on a separate piece of paper what each item means: a piece of grain, to represent the Goddess Brid, creativity, fertility, and good fortune; a garnet for love, whether love of self, family, or partner; a lodestone (lodestone acts as a magnet; if you pick the lodestone, you must also pick whatever item is nearest in order to receive your message of the future); an old key, to represent secrets to be revealed; an egg-shaped stone, to represent the coming month of March; a red feather, for passion; a black feather, for things to come; a white feather, to send away incorrect energy; and a blue feather, for happiness. A scrying box can contain any items you wish, charged with intentions you choose. You can include items that bring only good messages or you can compile a mixture of items that bring both good tidings and bad. An amazonite, a bluish, turquoise-colored stone, could bring a warning about health, for example. Scour antique stores or mystical shops to find small bottles or crystals and runes to include in your magical box. Once you have written down what each item stands for, ask a question. Shake the box and pick an object. You can choose as many items as you wish until you discern an answer from the messages inside.

SPRING EQUINOX
(around March 21st)

As I experience Spring Equinox, the dramatic moment each year when night and day are of equal length everywhere on the planet, I am reminded of the newness of our human family and of the ancient relationship between Earth, Sun, Moon, and sky. The turning of the Wheel of the Year is timeless and never-ending. The seasons, planetary movements, and tides triumphantly renew themselves, encoded as they are with the precedent of creation. As humans we awaken to our common origins, but stand in awe before the unanswerable mysteries of the universe. For Witches, Spring Equinox is an enchanted borderland time outside of time, where a magical seam joins dark with light. From this moment on, the Sun God begins His seminal journey across the sky, His light and warmth overtaking the darkness of Winter until His power peaks at Summer Solstice in June.

The influence of Spring Equinox upon the human experience is generous, dramatic, and profound. This subtle change from dark to light sends the exquisite message to all here on Earth that Springtime is the season of rebirth. At last we have arrived at the point on the Wheel when the Maiden Goddess becomes Mother once more, giving birth to the power of the Sun. As the melting snow and ice gives way to the green petals and delicate blooms of early Springtime flowers, I, too, feel a sense of renewal and joy. Febru-

ary's promise of a fresh beginning has been kept by Mother Earth. In return, I honor Her by giving thanks and praise to the pagan Goddess Ostera and the Faery Queen Blodeuwedd (pronounced *blod-oo-eeth).*

The Celtic people of Britain, Scotland, Ireland, and Wales engendered many other tribes. There is evidence of their influence in the traditions, myths, and practices of the peoples of Europe, Eastern Europe, the Mediterranean, Asia, India, and beyond. Ostera is a German pagan Goddess hailing from the Teutonic tribes. She is Goddess of Fertility and Rebirth. Indeed, to reveal the origins of the Christian celebration of Easter, which takes place on the first Sunday after the first full moon after Spring Equinox, we need look no farther than Ostera's ancient image. Ostera, which is often spelled Eostre, stands amid the flowers and vines of Spring holding an egg in her hand. Birds fly overhead and a rabbit hops playfully at her feet. Ostera and the egg she carries are symbols of newborn life.

The Welsh Blodeuwedd is Goddess of Earth's Renewal and Faery Queen Giver of Life. She is called Flower-Face and is one in a long line of Flower Women revered by the Celts and created in the Otherworld. Guinevere, who marries King Arthur, is also a Flower Woman. The patches of white clover we see in grass and fields in Spring are said to mark a Flower Woman's path. Blodeuwedd's face and hair are made of Spring flowers. Her dress, made from the mystical waters of the ninth wave, sparkles in the sunlight as it runs the length of her to become Tara, the Earth, at her feet. She is Goddess of Fertility, but also of Innocence, Enchantment, and the Dawn. In Celtic mythology, Blodeuwedd is changed into an owl and therefore she is also a symbol of wisdom and the waxing moon. Both Blodeuwedd and Ostera herald the arrival of Spring and are considered by

Witches to be necessary to the continuation of life here on Earth.

EARTH MAGIC

Spring Equinox is a time of new fire. The light and dark are in perfect balance, but the light is growing and the Sun is about to burst forth with new energy. The Hare Moon will wax full in April, but for now, the last days of March begin a season of fertility and growth. Spring Equinox is seeding time, a time when we begin to act on all we psychically planned at Samhain. In some regions we are able to plant the seeds we charged and anointed at Imbolc. In colder areas, however, we must continue to nurture plants and seedlings indoors, waiting until Beltane to plant. I am unable to plant my own garden until Beltane because of the colder weather in New England. At Spring Equinox, I do place an altar in the garden with three crystals and a potion for growth. I also keep images of the Sun God facing my garden to encourage His light and heat.

During this time of year, I often reflect upon how easy it is to go about doing the same old things in life over and over again without ever awakening to the world around us. There are people who live where I do, in Salem, Massachusetts, who have never been to Boston just forty minutes away. Many of us go through life seeing only what goes on in our own small worlds. We know and feel comfortable with our families, friends, and town, but have trouble relating to changes and events that take place in our states, countries, or world. Too often we see the "bigger picture" as irrelevant or out of our reach. We take for granted the patterns that we build in our lives, until something from the larger world around us comes along to interfere and disrupt our routines. A drought, for example, translates for many people as no water available to water the lawn. An oil shortage ends up in petty arguments in line at the gas pump. Because we are so focused on what is happening in our immediate surroundings, we often don't see our part in larger, global problems.

The reason behind all of our magic—the rituals, observances, meditations, and spellwork—is to constantly remind us that we *are* a factor in the larger scheme of things. Anything we do on an individual level affects the whole. Recycle everything that is able to be recycled. Don't let the faucet run in the sink. If you have a leak, get it fixed as soon as possible. Don't litter. When you go to the market, bring your own bag to carry groceries, or ask for plastic. Plastic can be recycled, but trees used to make paper bags cannot be.

Around the time of Spring Equinox, I often try to imagine everyone pitching in and taking part in their responsibility to the planet. During this time of year, when the light from the Sun is growing stronger and the ground softens from the warmth and melting snow, there are many ways to reseed the Earth and replenish the soil. If you are eating a piece of fruit, take the seeds or core and push them into the ground. Or save them in the freezer for a week or two so you can spread lots of seeds at once, giving the trees a better chance to grow. A friend and I scattered a bunch of peach seeds in a lot behind a café in our town, and now—just like magic!—we have a peach tree there. Whenever I go on car trips I bring snacks like sunflowers, rose hips, and fruit seeds to toss out the window along roadsides and highways. These are foods that are useful and healthful to people, animals, and birds. If everyone planted sunflowers along roadsides, there would be food for all.

Sometimes as a part of the ritual for Spring Equinox, we

replenish and enrich the soil with compost we've made ourselves in the weeks prior to our celebration. I do this regularly in my flower garden to make the soil rich and loamy. To make compost, simply store one or two weeks' worth of vegetable garbage and save it in a plastic bag in the freezer. I save my potato peelings, onion skins, celery ends—any kind of organic, biodegradable table scraps. When the ground is soft enough, go outside and dig a hole about a foot deep. I suggest buying a posthole digger, because it makes a neater hole and is good for minicomposting between plants. Bury your vegetable mixture, alternating between peelings and dirt until you fill the hole. I dig many holes, creating several minicomposts throughout the garden. If you do not have a garden, or do not own land, go into the woods or go to a park or vacant lot to give your gift to the Earth. This is a simple way we can each make a difference. Compost replenishes the soil and reduces our garbage. Imagine if we each did this once a month or even once a year in our cities, towns, and countrysides. Should a natural disaster of some kind strike, we would be ensured at least of rich, healthy soil in which to grow something we could eat.

Preparations

Spring Equinox is a fire time, but the fire is new and not full-blown. We combine cold colors of Winter with warm colors of Summer to create the cool shades of Spring. Lavender, for example, blends the blue of ice with a little red from fire. Green, the predominant shade of Spring Equinox and favorite color of the Faeries, combines blue with the yellow from the Sun. At Spring Equinox, reds are softened to pinks and dusty rose, blues to lavenders and violets, and bright yellows to soft canary yellow. The altar cloth is usually green. We decorate the altar in pastel shades using Spring flowers and new grasses.

For the ritual below you will need the following: small plants or seeds from Imbolc; flowers like jonquils, tulips, violets, or daffodils; rich dirt in a bowl; a white, a black, a yellow, a light green, a pink, and a red candle; a chalice; a ritual wand; Faery Fire Oil (see p. 96), Blodeuwedd's Oil and Ostera Oil (see p. 124), Flower-Face Philtre (see p. 123), and Springtime Protection Incense (see p. 124); rabbit fur from a live, shedding rabbit; painted eggs, enough for all who participate; and a freshly cut elder stick.

What to Wear

For Spring Equinox, we wear green, black, lavender, sky-blue, or pink robes, in fabrics that are cooler, such as cotton. Because the juices are returning to the branches in trees, flower crowns are easier to make. Twigs from Spring trees are pliable and entwine easily to make flower crowns. You also should wear makeup. The Celts were well known for making up their faces. Many tribes painted their entire bodies blue. At Spring Equinox we color our cheeks pink for a flower and make up our eyelashes like the petals of a flower. Often people paint their faces with flowers or use their entire face as the flower's center, painting the flower's petals aroung the edges of their face. Use a black eyebrow pencil to draw designs on your forehead or cheeks. Keep the eyebrow pencil in the freezer overnight so it can be sharpened without breaking. Over a makeup base on your forehead and cheeks draw spirals, knotwork, flowers, or triangles for the Triple Goddess. You can put powder over the designs so they look bluish like a tattoo.

The Ritual

Ideally, one should fast for three days before the Spring Equinox rite. If this is impossible, try to fast for at least six to twelve hours before the ritual. Here is a spring tonic to sip while fasting:

2 cups apple juice
2 cups spring water
½ cup carrot juice
2 sprigs thyme
½ cup lemon juice

Heat in a saucepan. Do not boil. Sip this tonic all the time while you fast, along with at least eight glasses of water during the three-day period. Break the fast with some kind of whole-grain bread.

Witches in the modern world often have a difficult time practicing their rituals because Witchcraft requires the presence of magic at the exact time of the changing of the Wheel, such as the Vernal Equinox in Spring. When the Sun's entry into Aries occurs, usually in the morning, some of us are asleep or at work, which means we must prepare ahead of time by asking our employers for the day off or leaving the exact ritual to the elders of the temple and then casting our own circle within the three-day grace of the event. The exact event, of course, offers the more powerful energy, and so the same power or energy will never again be displayed. You might remember equinoxes of the past, but each one is different.

A CALENDAR! A CALENDAR!

So many people who do not live in the northern hemisphere ask me by phone or write to me about how to practice the

Craft in their part of the world. Should they follow the seasons or should they follow along with the January-to-December Julian calendar? I often wondered about this myself. Years ago, after my divorce, I thought I was going to move to Australia and I wondered what I would do. After all, it's hot in December and January in Australia, so why would I want to do spellwork and rituals that project for warmth, the healing Sun, or protection? It is my belief that those living in the southern hemisphere should follow the ways of the Craft according to the seasons and not to the modern calendar. Witchcraft is about following Nature and connecting with Mother Earth on her own terms. Therefore, in February, those who live below the Equator would be celebrating Lughnasadh; Beltane in October, and Samhain in May. Follow the seasons and your own instincts, not someone else's Christianized version of a calendar.

Equinox circles are best done out-of-doors. A friend of mine owns a beautiful farm near the sea with sheep, cows, horses, and two llamas. This farm is a budding conservation land, so as you can imagine, it is the perfect place to do equinox magic. The sound of the birds and the fresh, sometimes cold air is refreshing. Last year we took a stroll on the farm. My companion, my daughters, and myself all sat down in the meadow. I curled up into my cape, enjoying the silence of the country and the singing of the birds. A Faery spell must have been cast upon us. We all fell asleep. We woke up some hours later to the sound of the soft snorting of a cow that had wandered over to get a good look at us. Naturally we got up, drew our circle in the Earth, and did our magic.

In New England some of our fiercest storms arrive in March. While it is important to get outside among Nature for this particular rite, many times we end up having to hold it indoors. This is acceptable, but not preferable. In any case, here is the ritual:

The High Priest casts the circle and the High Priestess anoints all candles with Ostera Oil, except for the red candle. She says: *I draw to this sacred space and land the power of the Goddess Ostera. I ask with the flickering of this flame that she comes to this Magic Circle.* She anoints the red candle with Faery Fire Oil and says: *O! precious Faery Queen Blodeuwedd, come to this place of magic. Bring to us the delights of Spring, the power of fertility, and the joy of beauty.*

The High Priest lights the charcoal and places incense on the charcoal. The High Priestess steps back and lifts her hands, holding a painted egg to the sky, and calls to Ostera: *O! Goddess of our ancestors, Ostera, bring your power to this world and renew all that is good for nature, the animals, the land, and humans that inhabit this space. Renew in all beings the ability to end pollution and destruction, to end disease and pain. Renew in us the power to be one with the choices you give us. You are blessed, Ostera.*

High Priest: *We hear the birds of Spring, the sounds of magic.*

The High Priestess picks up a bunch of flowers and says: *O! mighty and beautiful Blodeuwedd, cast the spell of beauty, health, and happiness to all here on Earth.*

She picks up the elder stick and touches it to the earth in the bowl and says: *I charge this wand and earth to empower the children of the Earth, to hear the call of the Faery Queen Blodeuwedd and the Goddess Ostera.*

This is a time of happiness and a time when we see the growth of flora.

The High Priestess plants some seeds in the bowl of earth. The High Priest lifts his blade as the High Priestess lifts the chalice of water. He touches the water with the blade and says: *I charge this water to stir and revive the seeds of life.* The High Priestess sips the water and says: *The waters of life.*

She pours some of the water into the bowl, watering the seeds. She hands the chalice to the High Priest and he says: *The waters of life.*

Both priest and priestess anoint themselves with Faery Fire Oil and they lift their hands up and say: *We are of the Faery faith. We are the children of the ancient ones. Their power is within our veins. We will renew this planet. We will stay aware of its sister Moon and father Sun. Blessed are the waters of life. So mote it be.*

The High Priestess holds the rabbit fur in her hands and charges it, asking Ostera to bless it with her magic. All present follow gestures of priest and priestess and raise their hands up to the sky and say: *We honor the God of light and the Goddess of beauty and might.*

High Priestess: *We send this magic to the winds of change. So mote it be.*

All bend down and touch the Earth. When all rise, the circle is undone, and the eggs are shared before moving on to the feast.

Magical Herbs

During this time of year, Witches use herbs and seeds to make the most of the wealth and healing warmth of the Sun. As on all holidays, at Spring Equinox we strive to carry the strength and goodness of the past into the newness of the coming season. We use herbs for protection and health, but also for growth, prosperity, love, and luck. Trefoil images representing the Triple Goddess have special meaning around this time of year. Any three-leaved grass is a gift from the Faeries bringing protection and luck. It is customary to leave a token of thanks to the Otherworld when you take a clover leaf or other three-leaved grass. In the North, the last days of March can sometimes be cold, rainy, and raw. This is still a season to bring life from outdoors inside. Budding crocuses or hyacinths will bloom inside, bringing the feeling of new Spring life into your home. I sometimes create mini rock gardens for my windowsills or altar, arranging twigs and stones and moss in a dish or special bowl. Moss is an excellent binder for spells. It brings moisture and freshness inside and is used in spells and philtres for attracting wealth. Vervain, one of the most sacred herbs for Witches, brings wealth, love, and protection and is said to be good for cleansing the blood as well. Honeysuckle is used for clarity of vision and creative inspiration in Spring.

Here is a list of herbs, seeds, and plants that are often used in the early Spring season:

lily of the valley
tansy
lavender
marjoram
thyme
tarragon
lovage
lilac
violets
lemon balm
dogwood

honeysuckle
oakmoss
orrisroot
apple, pear, peach seeds
sunflower seeds
rose hips
morning dew
oak
elder
willow
crocus

daffodil
jonquil
tulip
broom, Scotch or Irish
meadowsweet
acorn
trefoil (purple clover)
vervain

Philtres, Incense, and Oils

The arrival of Spring brings a renewed sense of energy to just about everyone on Earth. The Sun shines brighter and longer, and there is so much activity in the air, bird song, fresh breezes, playful gusts of wind, that we sometimes find ourselves growing tired before the day is done. Protecting our health is important now, and so is clearing the air for future Springtime activities and relationships. Witches often burn broom in incense to purify and protect. Burning broom blossoms and stems also changes the weather, either soothing the wind or stirring it up. You must not change weather for selfish reasons, however, for changing the weather in one part of the world affects the weather patterns of the entire planet. Vervain and moss are used in philtres and incense to resolve conflicts that may arise amid the frenetic energy and forces of Spring. Often on Spring mornings I go outside to collect the morning dew from the grass and leaves on the trees. Morning dew is for power and is often used in oils to enhance their magical intent.

FLOWER-FACE PHILTRE

dried lavender
dried violets
dried apples
meadowsweet
broom
clover

Blend all ingredients in a magic bowl or bag.

OSTERA OIL

1 dram almond oil
1 dram patchouli
1 dram elder oil
1 dram lavender oil
1 dram violet oil

Warm all ingredients in an enamel saucepan. Remove from heat. Let cool. Keep in green, blue, pink, or lavender bottles.

BLODEUWEDD'S OIL

1 dram lily of the valley
1 dram violet oil
1 dram honeysuckle oil
lemon balm

(Same instructions as above)

SPRINGTIME PROTECTION INCENSE

1 part each of the following:

patchouli
lavender
vervain

Place all ingredients in a magic bowl or bag with Springtime colors. To charge, bring into your sacred space or Magic Circle during the ritual.

Magical Stones

During this time of year, we strive to achieve the ideal balance represented by the Spring Equinox. Stones, like trees, are our books from which we gain knowledge and spiritual guidance. When dealing with stones, handle them with care. Feel their weight and vibration in the palm of your hand. Do you prefer certain stones over others? Are the colors found in one stone more pleasing to your eye than the colors of another? When you discover what colors and sizes and shapes of stones are right for you, you can use them in a variety of magical ways. Witches use stones for meditation. In philtres they help to increase the power of enchantment. During Springtime, we wear stones as amulets or talismans for strength, centering, protection, and good fortune. Stones arranged in circles or facing the four directions draw in and emit more power and magical energy. White stones tend to bring balance to our lives and help point us down the correct paths. Green stones usually signify growth, healing, and success.

Here is a list of stones I often use in my magic around this time of year:

clear quartz crystal
rose quartz
agate
lapis lazuli
amazonite
garnet

Magical Spells

Spring is also a time for planting ideas. In Spring our minds soar with plans for our careers, relationships, and love. We call on Blodeuwedd, Goddess of the Mysterious Moon, so that we may foretell the future correctly. We ask her to help us make our dreams and hopes reality. Around this time of year I often meditate on the nesting of new birds, and on the new growth of plants, flowers, and vines. Just as the birds build their nests, many of us often feel like redecorating our homes or offices. At Spring Equinox I leave locks of my hair in the trees in my garden to help the birds in creating their own homes for their babies. Rabbit fur, representing fertility and growth, is often used in Springtime spells as quickening. In my own spellwork I seek to be brought into balance and harmony with the incredible energy of the season, and I project for good health, good fortune, and confidence in achieving my goals. Here are some spells you might want to try.

SPRING CLEANING MEDITATION

We often hold on to emotional and spiritual debris, keeping it locked away until soon it becomes spiritual clutter. Here is a meditation to help you do some spiritual spring cleaning. Go into alpha. Picture yourself cleaning an old attic filled with antique glass dishes, pretty old furniture, and trunks. See the cobwebs hanging down from the rafters and dust on everything. Go to a window at the end of the attic and open it. Feel the cool, fresh air beginning softly to enter the attic. Take your magic Witch's broom and begin to sweep. Then pick up the piles of dust and toss them out the window. Take a magic wand and touch the furniture, glass, and trunks. See them all clean and dusted. All dust, cobwebs, and dirt fly out the window. Take a polishing crystal and touch each object until it is clean and shining. There is a full-length mirror in the corner. Stand in front of it and you will see that you have cleaned everything but yourself. Just like in the story of Cinderella, you wave your wand and the dust and cobwebs in your hair are gone. Your hair is shiny and beautiful, your skin is radiant and clean, your teeth sparkle, and your clothing becomes new. Now you look into your spirit and aura. You may see cobwebs and dust. If you do, use your magic broom, wand, and crystal. Touch all the cobwebs in your spirit, body, and brain. Make sure everything is bright, clean, and shining, and glowing with a brilliant light. Anytime you feel you have cobwebs, dust, and clutter in your spirit and life, sit down and do this meditation.

SPRING EQUINOX SPELL

This is a spell to increase your wealth and earning powers. You will need:

1 pink, 1 blue, and 1 white candle
1 peyton
1 charcoal and thurible
Springtime Protection Incense (see p. 124)
Faery Fire Oil (see p. 96)
Ostera Oil (see p. 124)
rabbit fur from a live, shedding rabbit
1 chalice filled with spring water
1 ritual blade or small wand
1 large bowl of warm water and a towel
2 lapis lazuli stones
1 garnet
1 amazonite
1 pink magic bag
1 blue magic bag
1 blue dyed or painted egg
1 magic mirror
1 blue pen
parchment

Set your altar and cast your circle, place the magic mirror beyond your thurible. Light your charcoal and place incense on it. Anoint pink, white, and black candles with Ostera Oil. Anoint your blue candle with Faery Fire Oil. It represents

Jupiter. The energy of Jupiter influences people in high places, expands careers and visions, and helps you to win.

Pick up your peyton or hold your hand out toward the North and say: *I call the element of Earth, the badger;* point to the East and say: *I call the element of Fire, the red fox;* point to the South and say: *I call the element of Air, the owl;* point to the West and say: *I call the element of Water, the salmon.*

Wash your hands in the warm water and dry them with the towel. Pick up the pen and write the following spell on the parchment:

"I ask in the name of the Goddess Ostera that I be granted a connection with the growth of Spring, that my earning powers be increased, my health improved, my spirit rise to the needs of my God and Goddess. So mote it be. I ask this to be correct in the plans of the God and Goddess and to be for the good of all."

Lift the small wand and touch it to the water in the chalice, saying: *I ask Ostera to enter this holy cup and charge this water with her energy that I may drink the waters of life.*

Then sip the water. Feel the Goddess Ostera entering your aura. She will help you to be more powerful and to achieve all she wishes for you and the good of the world. Touch the blue egg with the wand. Then speak your spell out loud. Sprinkle incense on the charcoal. Pass the spell through the smoke. Touch the stones and the rabbit fur with the wand and charge them with the energy of Ostera. Anoint them with her oil. Place the stones in the magic bag. The pink one is to carry on yourself. The other is to place or hang in your living space. Sit and gaze into your magic mirror. Ask Ostera to show you a sign or symbol that you will use to enhance your magic until Beltane. Say this into the mirror: *Magic mirror show to me what my symbol is to be.*

After you have released the circle, keep your spell with you. Do not burn it. Every time you think of the things you have asked for, picture in your mind the symbol you received in your magic mirror. If you wish, you can draw the symbol on a piece of parchment or on the spell you are carrying.

HOLIDAY FARE

The fresh, clean breezes of early Spring bring with them savory new aromas from the kitchen. Spring lamb is young and tender now, and vegetables are beginning to taste better and feel firmer and fresher. The cream and milk of Imbolc are still a part of the holiday meal, but eggs play a more prominent role in all foods eaten around this time of year. In his wonderful book *The Magic of Food,* Scott Cunningham writes, "According to one belief, eggs are the perfect symbols of creation. Not only do they produce life itself (if they are fertilized), but the shell represents Earth; the membrane, Air; the yolk, Fire; and the white, Water." The egg is the beginning of life and considered to be so magical it represents the mysteries of the beginnings of the entire universe and all we see in the world.

During our Spring Equinox celebrations, we use eggs in practically all meals. For breakfast, we make delicious omelets and poached eggs using herbs like tansy, dill, and parsley. We often bake bread with a decorated egg inside. We use violets to enhance fruits and add sparkle to early Spring salads garnished with hard-boiled eggs. The Feast of Ostera is a time to give thanks for the fertility and growth the Mother and Sun have so generously produced. Following are a few suggestions of what to serve:

Feast of Ostera

Posset (Hot Milk Punch)
Roasted Spring Lamb with Herbs
Green Man Salad with Green Dressing
Stuffed Ostera Eggs
Candied Ostera Eggs

POSSET (HOT MILK PUNCH)

1 qt. whole milk
1 tsp. grated lemon rind
½ cup sugar
5–6 ground almonds
2 egg whites
½ cup dark rum
1 cup brandy

In a saucepan warm milk, lemon rind, and sugar. Just before milk mixture begins to boil, add almonds and remove from burner. Beat well and gently blend in egg whites. Add rum and brandy and stir until frothy. Serve in a charged cauldron.

ROASTED SPRING LAMB WITH HERBS

5-lb. leg of lamb
butter
garlic, slivered
lemon
basil
thyme
tarragon
chives
1 cup dry red or white wine
2 shallots
milk or cream
flour

Rub sides of roasting pan with butter so drippings won't burn. Place roast fat side up and rub with garlic for protection, lemon for the Sun, basil for love, and the remaining herbs. Make tiny slits in the roast, inserting slivers of garlic. Halfway through roasting add wine, shallots, and more herbs to taste. Roast 30 minutes to the pound at 350° F. Remove roast. Boil and reduce drippings or thicken with milk or cream and flour.

GREEN MAN SALAD WITH GREEN DRESSING

zucchini
greens
cucumbers
watercress

Toss all ingredients in a salad bowl. Dress with lemon and honey or Green Dressing: 1 cup mayonnaise, 1/4 cup pesto, a pinch of watercress, poppy seeds, and a dash of vinegar.

STUFFED OSTERA EGGS

Eating eggs at Spring Equinox is equivalent to ingesting the energy of Ostera.

8 eggs, hard-boiled
2 cups mayonnaise
1/8 cup sugar
1/2 cup vinegar or sweet gherkin juice
fresh thyme or basil
watercress

Peel eggs and slice lengthwise, end to end. Scoop out egg yolks and mash or blend in a blender. Add mayonnaise, sugar, and vinegar. Whip until creamy. Refill egg whites with mixture, using a pastry bag or carefully placing mixture in with a teaspoon. Garnish with fresh thyme or basil, if desired, and put watercress underneath on the dish.

CANDIED OSTERA EGGS

In both ends of 8 eggs, poke pinholes. Blow in one end until egg is emptied out. Tape one hole shut and open the other to the size of a nickel. Wash the eggshell, rinse, and place back in egg carton. Melt milk chocolate or Nestlé crunch bars over low heat. Pour chocolate into eggshells. Refrigerate until chocolate hardens. To eat, peel off outside shell.

ANCIENT ACTIVITIES

The ancient tradition of coloring eggs in Springtime was practiced by the Celts, but was elevated to an exquisite art form by the tribes of Eastern Europe. Ukraine, in particular, has been admired for untold centuries for their remarkable designs. One Spring, before the fall of the Berlin Wall, a young girl who had defected from the Soviet Union showed up on my doorstep to sell me her eggs. These were the only things she was able to carry with her, and now they were standing her in good stead, helping her to earn money to get by in her new world. The black eggs were gorgeously decorated in traditional designs. I bought as many as I could afford and gave many away to members of my coven.

Witches usually do not dye their eggs, but paint them with symbols, runes, and banded designs. The Celts painted their eggs a scarlet red to symbolize the burning Sun. A green egg with a serpent wrapped around symbolizes fertility and the birth of the universe. An apple is the sacred symbol of the Witch and a dragon is often used to represent Merlin the Magician.

A variety of dyes can be made using the roots of certain herbs and peels from vegetable skins. Five or six stems of madder root or gorse blossom will make red, for example.

Use less than this amount to achieve a light pink. Make yellow from turmeric root, found in the spice aisle at the market and a blue from woad seeds or leaves. The Celts used to paint their faces and bodies with dye made from woad. Boil onion peel for a light orange. Carrot tops yield a pale yellow-green, and coltsfoot or bracken produce green. Red cabbage leaves and vinegar or crushed blueberries or blackberries create a blue and gray-blue.

Following is a list of some of the more common symbols and their meanings that Witches paint on eggs:

Sun: Young God, Bel, God of Light, Inspiration
Moon: Triple Goddess, Lunar Mysteries
Stars: Silver Wheel, Goddess Arianrhod
Ram's Horns: Horned God, Nature's Life Force, Fertility
Deer or Stag: Prosperity, Fertility, Horned God
Encircling Bands: Magic Circle, Wheel of the Year, Eternal Cycle of Life
Rake or Hoe: Agricultural Growth
Waves: the Element of Water
Oak Tree: Oak King, Merlin, Strength, Wisdom
Flowers: Blodeuwedd

Egg Hunt

After you've painted or dyed your eggs and decorated them with symbols with different meanings, hide them. If weather permits, hide them outside, but in some parts of the world around this time of year it is often too cold to enjoy the outdoors for too long. Children and adults both enjoy a good egg hunt, but if you were only able to decorate a limited number of eggs, the hunting is best left up to the children. The symbols and runes on the eggs they find tell auguries for the future. As a prize, we often give a potted tree named after the child who finds the most eggs.

When I was a little girl, I remember one year an egg hunt my father devised for us during the Spring Equinox season. We were in Oklahoma visiting relatives when my father woke me early in the morning. We all hopped into his old touring car and rambled off down a few dirt roads until he cut off the road and turned into a stream. We splashed along, the car straddling the brook the entire way, until the stream opened up into a beautiful sunlit meadow sparkling in morning dew. This is where we hunted for eggs.

Looking back on it, I realize that Spring Equinox was a magical time of year for my family. My mother, though not a Witch, was to my mind touched by the Faeries and in tune with and sensitive to the ways of enchantment. Every year, she would place black velvet under my basket of eggs and candy. The night before, she would dip my cat's paws in talcum powder to make "bunny" footprints on the velvet. I was so enchanted by this. I thought the bunny really came to my house every year, and to this day, I'm not so sure she doesn't!

Faery Magic

As the last days of Winter are carried away by the chilly winds of March, we look to the Faery World for omens of Spring. There is an old expression: "Keep your eye on the bunny and the bird," which is a Faery expression meaning that the answers you seek are often found in Nature. Crows, for example, are favorable signs of a good crop. In Spring it is usually a good idea to feed the crows so they do not eat your crop. Birds and rabbits, of course, bring messages of growth and a promising Spring. Circles of mushrooms, which we often see in Spring and Summer, are Faery Rings and places of great power and magic.

Frequently around this time of year, Witches invoke or call upon the Faery deity known as the Green Man. The Green Man embodies the spirit of growth and magic found in Nature and is a sacred God of the woods and trees. He has many associations with the Celtic and British Horned God Cernunnos. The Horned God symbolizes the masculine side of Nature. He, too, is God of the Woods, and takes on many forms. He is the God Hearne, whom we met at Yule in the form of the Stag. In Spring, Cernunnos opens the floodgates of life.

The balance and perfect circle of the wheel is also given to us by the Faeries and is an important image around this time of year. In ancient times, as part of the Spring Equinox ritual, a wheel of fire was hurled from atop the sacred hill of the Faeries, where festivities were usually held. This practice continued in some areas up until the eighteenth century. The original fire wheels were symbols of the Celtic Cross, a magic circle with spokes representing the four directions and the four elements. This is also the fire wheel of the burning Sun.

Spring is a great time to be outside and in touch with your natural surroundings. Here is a spell that will help you better appreciate the magic of trees:

Sacred Tree Spell

You will need:

- *1 white, 1 black, 1 green, and 1 yellow candle*
- *1 ash pot*
- *1 thurible and charcoal*
- *Springtime Protection Incense (see p. 124)*

Ostera Oil (see p. 124)
Faery Fire Oil (see p. 96)
3 sprigs or small branches from a sacred tree
1 magic wand or sword
1 chalice with spring water
1 bowl of earth salt and sea salt combined
4 green satin ribbons, each 2 yards long
1 red, 1 pink, 1 lavender ribbon
1 clear quartz crystal
1 amazonite
1 rose quartz
1 bowl with spring water
parchment
pink pen

Set your altar and cast your circle. Light the charcoal and sprinkle incense on it. Place the salt bowl to your left and the bowl with water to your right. Anoint the candles with Ostera Oil and say: *Ostera, strike this flame with your might, Goddess of the day and night.*

Place three twigs on your altar where you can reach them. Raise your wand and say: *Ostera, Goddess of Spring, O! Green Man, God of Growth, come to my sacred land. Empower me and guide my hand.*

Use your pink pen and write this spell:

"Green Man, grant to me the future that I now can see. You are the creation of the Great Mother. She gives air, the breath of life. She gives water, the waters of life. She gives food, the sustenance of life. She gives passion, the spark of life."

Place three drops of Ostera Oil and Faery Fire Oil in the bowl of water. Pick up each ribbon one by one, hold the pink ribbon first and say: *This ribbon sets to time self-love and it is mine.* Dip it in the bowl of water. Take the lavender ribbon: *This ribbon balance gives, so Mother Earth lives.* Dip it into the bowl of water. Take the red ribbon and say: *Red, the fire of Faeryland, heals the Earth by my hand.* Dip it into the water. Pick up four green ribbons together and say: *Green Man! Green Man! Your powers be to set this spell upon the tree.* Dip them in the water.

Take three sprigs of sacred tree and touch with your wand. Touch the salt and then your chalice and say: *Waters of life, grant to me the powers of the living tree.* Take a sip of the water and save the rest. Read the spell out loud. Light it afire with the green candle and place it in the ash pot to burn. As it burns, visualize the spells coming to be. Touch the wand to the crystals to charge them. Release your circle.

Take the bowl of salt water, ashes, and ribbons to the sacred tree outside. Leave the salt in a bowl at the base of the tree, sprinkle ashes around the tree, bury your crystal in the dirt under the base of the tree or balance it somewhere in one of the branches. One by one tie your ribbons onto the tree branches and remember your spells, to reinforce them, and the tree will do your magic for you.

BELTANE
(May 1st)

In the Otherworld, on the Eve of Beltane each year, a foal is stolen by a great claw from the stable of a man named Tiernon. One May Eve, Tiernon decides to chase the thief. He retrieves the foal and returns to the stable to find a baby boy swaddled in a blanket. He brings up the boy as his own, and the horses become the boy's friends. As the boy matures, however, Tiernon realizes he is the Goddess Rhiannon's abducted son and returns him to his mother.

When her son was first discovered missing, Rhiannon was wrongly accused by the baby's nursemaids of having eaten the boy. She is sentenced to stand for seven years in front of the great hall, offering to carry upon her back all who wish to enter. She must also tell her story to anyone who will listen. When at last her lost son is restored to her, Rhiannon says "At last my trouble is over." She then names the boy Pryderi, which means "trouble."

Rhiannon's name translates as "the Great Queen." She is a Great Goddess from the Welsh tribes, who rides a white horse and is able to shapeshift into a horse that is faster than any other. She meets her future husband and Pryderi's father, Pwyll, at the sacred Faery hill, the Mound of Arberth in Wales. He chases her on his horse, but her horse is always faster. When she decides to stop, Rhiannon chooses Pwyll for her mate. She tells him she has been promised to someone else without her consent and that she loves Pwyll. A year and a day later, Pwyll shows up at Rhiannon's father's home. He gains the hand of Rhiannon, but only thanks to her quick thinking and magical expertise, for Rhiannon gives Pwyll a magical bag in which to trap her former betrothed. United, they return to his kingdom to rule. Because she has not as yet given birth to a son, Rhiannon is not well liked by the people of Pwyll's land. She eventually does give birth, but her son is stolen in his infancy (only to be discovered by Tiernon in the stable) and Rhiannon is sentenced to her punishment.

The theme of the Great Mother and her Son, who is either lost or stolen and then returned to become his Mother's hero, occurs over and over again in Celtic mythology. Though Rhiannon can be invoked or called upon at any point on the Wheel of the Year, I often find myself reflecting upon her story and her amazing gifts at either Beltane or Samhain. These are the two times of the year when the veil between the two worlds is thinnest, a time revered and cherished by the Celts. The Celts divided the year not into four seasons, but into two, Winter and Summer. Beltane marks that turning point in time, which is on the edge of time, when Winter is over and Summer about to begin.

For me, Rhiannon's story reveals so many of the themes that the festival of Beltane represents. Rhiannon is bringer and joiner of both darkness and light, happiness and tragedy, death, life, and rebirth. Rhiannon bears many burdens for the benefit of her people and the land. When her son is returned she feels a great relief. Just as her troubles are over, by May 1st, so too are our own. The dark time of year, with all of its Winter woes, by Beltane is a distant memory. The barrenness of Winter eventually ends as Rhiannon's barrenness ends with the birth of her son. In myth, whenever

Rhiannon and Pryderi suffer, the land suffers, because she is Earth and he, the Sun. Whenever they are reunited, the land rejuvenates, full-blown with life, and even more lush and abundant than before. Beltane brings us to that time on the Wheel of the Year when life is good—and sweeter than we ever could have imagined in Winter.

EARTH MAGIC

The word *Beltane* simply means "fire of Bel." Bel is the "bright or shining one." The Romans called him Belanos, but his roots can also be linked to Baal from Asia, which means "god." In modern Irish, Beltane means May. In his honor, on the eve of May first, the ancient Celts set two large fires using nine of the sacred woods. (See Sacred Trees of the Celts, p. 267.) On this night animal herds were ritually driven between the two fires to purify and protect them from disease and harm. From there they were sent to Summer pastures until the following Samhain, when they would once again return to their pens for wintering in.

On Beltane, Witches celebrate the great fruitfulness of the Earth. In our rite we light a Beltane fire symbolically in a cauldron, using the sacred woods just as our ancestors did. If we have the space, we light a large fire more in keeping with tradition. In ritual we celebrate the union between the Great Mother and her young Horned God. Their coupling brings fresh new life on Earth, which we each experience in the exuberance of Spring.

Beltane is the season to "go a-maying." May, the fifth month in numerology, is a month of sensuality and sexual revitalization. Our five senses are particularly sharp in May. Love is in the air. On this day, couples may decide to live together for a year and a day to see if they can find a rich and loving life. After a year and a day they may decide to part company. This concept of "marriage" is an acceptable idea to the Craft. I believe it takes time for one person to know another. We do not vow to live our lives together "until death do us part." Witches understand the ways of nature, though we always strive for the best love and family life we can have with mutual love and trust. In relationships, people grow, learn, and sometimes change their personalities entirely. By living with another person and experiencing the education a relationship has to offer, couples are often able to broaden their visions about careers, talents, and goals. Entering into a year-and-a-day handfast helps all parties involved. Each can go into the union without feeling trapped. They know that they may choose not to continue, gifting the relationship with both freedom and strength at the same time.

Children of handfastings are not considered to be without parents. Girls always keep their mother's last name. If a couple has a boy, he would keep his mother's name but use his father's name last. My two daughters have my last name. My grandson has his father's last name and his mother's name hyphenated. By this arrangement no one loses their lineage and the mother's line or heritage is as powerful as the father's.

May Eve is a time of preparation for May Day. One year, while visiting England, I was invited to join my friends' coven for the Beltane celebration. I awoke at daybreak May Eve and opened the leaded windows that looked out upon a field of grazing cattle. I heard muffled laughter and giggling. I looked farther out the window and saw my hosts in the garden splashing each other with branches covered in fresh dew. It is said that if you bathe in May Eve morning dew, you will have a beautiful complexion. I ran downstairs, washed my face, and went outside to join them.

Some of the coven began arriving. They were carrying large baskets and bunches of every flower abloom in the English countryside. There were violets and primroses, wallflowers and poppies. I had never seen so beautiful an array of Spring flowers. We brought them into the kitchen and set about making wreaths and crowns for the gathering. The warm sunrise was shining and I could hear the birds in the meadows. Sitting in that thatched-roof cottage near the Tor was a romantic, magical time for me. I felt as if I were in our holy land, Summerland.

Off on a hill, members of the group were preparing a Bel fire, using oak, holly, and the rest of the sacred woods. The fire was to be lit at twilight. The sweet scent of flowers made my head light and we all felt the flirtatious spell of Spring. After completing our floral crowns we took time to drive into the fields and touch the standing stones nearby, knowing that the power of Spring was full-blown. That evening was spent singing, feasting, dancing, and watching the flames on the hill.

The next day I was so excited to participate in their Beltane circle and watch the maypole dance. The children had no need for practice. They had done this all their lives. Some of the hot coals were brought down from the hills and kept in a cauldron for all to jump over before the maypole dance. Many older people held branches of flowering trees and began to dance around, striking the ground with the branches to hurry up Spring and wake up the land.

Preparations

Green is the color of Beltane. The altar should be draped in green cloth and decorated with blooming flowers and herbs. For this ritual you will need a crown of spring flowers, a chalice of spring water, an athame or blade, a cauldron, twigs from the list of sacred woods (see p. 267), and altar matches.

What to Wear

The Celts were extremely interested in ornamentation and were very fancy in their dress. Although many practitioners of the Craft, particularly followers of Alexandrian and Gardnerian Witchcraft, perform their rituals skyclad, or nude, practicing in this manner is not necessarily a part of the Celtic tradition, where Witchcraft began. Naturism, or practicing nude, is one man's view of the Craft. Gerald Gardner brought this interpretation to our religion, just as I brought the emphasis on science. While I respect these views, I do not adhere to them. To my mind, if energy is able to penetrate walls and travel distances between planets and suns, it can penetrate clothing and fully affect my body, spirit, and mind. Wearing clothing, jewelry, and makeup was important to our Celtic ancestors. They wore crowns, headdresses, gauntlets, robes, tartans, and vestments in vibrant colors such as scarlets, blues, violets, greens, browns, and reds. The Celts have a long history of making fabric. Weaving, knotwork, and sewing are intrinsic to our magic. We weave spells and sew magical symbols that are rich with meaning upon our clothing. Celtic jewelry rivals that of the Egyptians and may even have inspired it.

At our Beltane festival we wear green robes, many-colored vestments, and floral crowns. Sometimes we braid flowers in our hair or don leafy green masks to represent the "green people," or Pan race, who have pointy ears and little horns. The legend of Robin Hood, who dressed in green from top to toe, symbolizes the return of gifts of things stolen from us by Winter. He is a green forest spirit and champion of the land and people.

RITUAL DANCE

Dance is a means by which we are bound to the past; it provides a reflection of our beliefs and faith. Dance is feeling the spirit. Most of us know instinctively how to dance. We have been dancing all our lives. It is in our blood. And when we as Witches perform our rituals, there is no set routine or wrong way of dancing. We enjoy the camaraderie and intensity we feel when our fellow Witches dance. We are sharing sensibilities. The movements of the dance, which can be lavish or resonantly simple, make us deeply conscious of the positive energies we strive to raise. In short it makes us feel good, feel bonded, and feel alive. It is celebrating our human experience of joy. Movements and gestures in dancing summon the kind of meaningful experience that links us with our purpose. There are many benefits derived from dancing during rituals. Some of the dances capture the flavor of a particular ritual with a blend of affection, devotion, and joy. Our dances are usually done in circles to music. At holidays, we have our own choir and musicians. If you are skilled at dance, you can really explore more sophisticated movements. But you can also simply step or sway. Every movement we perform suggests and enhances our awareness of each other and our purpose, to honor and love our Mother the Earth, the Moon, and the sky.

The Ritual

In the Beltane ritual, the elders of the temple often choose a young female to represent the May Queen and a young male to represent the conquering king. She is crowned with flowers and clothed in a green cape or robe. He is crowned with stag horns and flowers to represent the Stag of Seven Tines, and dresses in green or white. The Stag of Seven Tines is the totem animal of the Horned God Cernunnos and symbolic of the life force in nature.

Composed by the Reverend High Priest Richard Ravish of the Temple of Nine Wells, the following ritual was spiritually inspired. Richard tells me that the pen began to shake in his hand as if someone else were writing through him. He transcribed the following ceremony:

> High Priest: *The light, long smothered by Winter's chill in Bel's halls beneath the Earth, is now set free. The Goddess Dana, once restrained by the dark season's lord, is now released from his hold. The seed of life buried in loam long ago springs forth anew. Think now on the never-ending cycle of light and darkness; how the light first blazes ever so bright, then sinks into the depths, dark, and nigh unto death, yea, snuffed unto death. We, the secret children of the Goddess on the verge of Summer, tender now our memories of Summer days and warmer seasons past.*
>
> High Priestess: *We call on our Earth Mother to return, to reclaim her domain and her throne of power. We call for the May Queen and bid her to answer her children's call.*
>
> (At this point another High Priestess who has been appointed is named Rhiannon and called by the first High Priestess.)
>
> High Priestess: *Rhiannon, step forward. How may we*

herald the return of our Goddess? How may we hasten the arrival of Spring? How may we initiate the magic of life's return and encourage Mother Dana to blanket the Earth with greenery and the warmth of love?

(High Priestess hands a crown that is green and decorated with flowers to Rhiannon.)

High Priestess: *Thus we mark this holy day. Thus we crown the Queen of May.*

(Rhiannon places the crown on her head.)

All participating respond in unison: *We light the Bel fire and call our Goddess forth. We bid great Dana to return to the lusty embrace of mighty Belenos, Sun God, O! Great God of shiny countenance and ruddy cheeks, let your flames melt our Goddess's heart once more. Let your love quicken the life within her womb.*

(A Bel fire is now set alight either on a hill or in a cauldron. The High Priestess invokes over the flaming cauldron.)

High Priestess: *Hear us, ye old ones. We call forth the Goddess Dana from her hidden realm, for this is the time she reclaims her power. We call to thee, O! Dana, Queen of May, Faery fair, Goddess of Moon and Earth. Thee, Great Star Goddess, come to us, great Dana, and share thy power. Return! Return! Return to your children who gather in thy name. O! Bride of the Sun, Earth Mother, return.*

(The High Priestess lifts the chalice. The High Priest lifts his athame.)

High Priest: *Belenos, Belenos, up from the South, we call thee. Sun God, who courses the heavens with chariot and steeds of fire, whose bow looses the arrow of sunlight, whose rays now beat once more upon the Earth and by turn nourish temperate breezes, favor us with blessings O! Great Sun God, in thy matings with the Goddess. Bring us joy and passion and bliss in sweet surrender. Pleasure our Goddess with Summer heat.*

(The High Priest turns the blade in the water three times. They each take a sip of the water and set it down. Now everybody jumps the flaming cauldron, singing the following song:)

Here we come a piping,
in Springtime and in May.
Green fruit aripening,
and Winter flood away.
The queen, she sits upon the strand,
fair as lily, white as wand.
Seven billows on the sea,
horses riding fast and free,
and bells upon the sand.

(After the ritual of jumping the cauldron, all participants dance around the maypole, singing the following song:)

May the balance be restored,
between the lady and the lord.
Earth below and sky above,
share the blessings of their love.

Magical Herbs

Herbs are such versatile and remarkable plants. During Spring we weave herbs and flowers into garlands and crowns to be esteemed for their beauty and used in our sacred rites. We often cook with budding herbs, and use their petals, stems, and leaves in healing medicines and potions to bring romance, fertility, and wealth. The herbs of

Beltane have the power to grip the imagination of a lover. The intoxicating blooms and aromas of fresh dogwood and daffodils, meadowsweet and rosemary, are delicious and so pleasing to the eye that we drift off into the sweet land of fantastic and luxuriant dreams. The savory scent of mint increases your Springtime lust for life and is good for the emotions of the heart. Strew meadowsweet or mint in your bedroom or sleeping space to keep the air fresh, titillate your senses, and make your heart glad. Rue is good for treating beestings, while the brave allheal has a long history of healing wounds, from cuts and scrapes to mortal gashes.

At Beltane, Witches often use herbs and plants ruled by Venus (for love) and Jupiter and the Sun (for prosperity). Hawthorn is a Faery bush and one of the many sacred woods. One must never cut one down or cut a piece without asking the Faeries' permission. Beltane is the only time of year on the Wheel that you can bring hawthorn into the house.

Here is a list of herbs to promote and foster love and romance, followed by a more general list of herbs to be used in incense, oils, and brews.

Love herbs for union:

broom
coriander
meadowsweet
rosemary
yarrow
almond
blessed thistle
mint

Beltane herbs:

allheal
daffodil
dogwood
coriander
blessed thistle
broom
curry
dragon's blood reed

fern	snapdragon
fireweed	mushroom
nettle	almond
flaxseed	meadowsweet
hawthorn	rose
marjoram	satyrian root
paprika	woodruff
radish	tansy
rue	elder leaves

Philtres, Incense, and Oils

Like Samhain, Beltane is a prime time for reaping the wisdom of our ancestors in the Otherworld. Rhiannon, Dana, and Bel help us glean much knowledge and pleasure from the invigorating Springtime season. Creating philtres, incense, and oils simply makes communicating with the Goddesses and Gods easier and more fun. During the Beltane season, Witches use a variety of blends to keep the air fresh and clean, attract romance, love, and success, and promote healing and protection. All proportions given below are flexible and should be adjusted to your personal preference using magical intent and aromatherapy as your guide. Fixatives or binders in philtres, incense, and oils help to maintain scent. In dry blends, pinch herbs to bring back an aroma that is fading. Here are a few concoctions that are used in magical spells and meditations discussed later in this chapter.

BELTANE PHILTRE

dried daffodil
coriander
nettle
flaxseed
mushroom
meadowsweet

Mix all ingredients and place in a magic bowl or bag.

BEL'S INCENSE

marjoram
nettle
broom
woodruff
2 drops Dana Oil (see below)

Mix all ingredients using a couple of drops of Dana Oil to bind it. Carry in a magic bag or store in a magic bottle or jar.

DANA OIL

1 dram almond oil
1 dram dragon's blood
½ dram rose oil
clear quartz crystal—just drop in
a few dried rose petals

Warm all ingredients in an enamel saucepan on very low heat. Let cool and place in a magic bowl or bottle to store.

RHIANNON OIL

1 dram dragon's blood oil
1 dram rue oil
1 pinch paprika
rose quartz

Heat in an enamel saucepan. Let cool and place in a magic bottle.

Magical Stones

Perhaps we are not being facetious when we speak of a love relationship as being "solid as a rock." Stones, gems, metals, and crystals have the ability to convey deep, unbending meaning to partners in a relationship. The stones of Beltane promote partnership, marriage, passion, and love, whether self-love, sexual love, or love for family and friends. As a High Priestess, I am recognized by the Commonwealth of Massachusetts as a minister of religion with the power to legally marry lovers in a traditional Handfasting Ceremony. During the ceremony, just as in many traditions, it is customary to exchange rings, whether bands of gold or rings studded with gems and crystals. Following is a list of stones often used in handfasting rites or to promote love in any relationship.

Stones for Handfasting:

malachite	beryl
garnet	tourmaline
rose quartz	copper
emerald	gold

Magical Spells

Every year, members from my coven travel to Glastonbury, England, to visit and perform the Beltane ritual at the Tor. One year, three coveners went dressed in their Celtic regalia, wearing exquisite gauntlets, chain mail, torques, and other forms of traditional ornamentation. As they made their way along the magical spiral trail to the top, three white horses crossed their path. They were speechless, greeting Rhiannon with awestruck silence. At the midway point, three rabbits appeared and led them up the path. They were Ostera, heralding the fertility of Spring. At the top, two lovers rustled awake from their May Eve sleep, leaning against the base of the tower in sleeping bags. Bel was about to arrive. The lovers watched surprised and misty-eyed, while the three coveners set up and prepared to perform the ritual at the exact moment of daybreak. One held a silk veil toward the East, the second the chalice, and the third a ritual blade over the chalice. The moment the blade pierced the silk, the first beam of sunlight from the break of dawn struck the blade and dashed through the opening in the veil. It was such a magical moment played out before an enchanted and sensual gathering of five—three Witches and two lovers.

The spiritual energy afoot on Beltane is powerful. Our rites and spellwork bring us strange and wonderful experiences around this time of year. Beltane brings bright expectations of the future, so it is a time for spells that ensure prosperity, conservation, safety, and love. Here are some spells you may want to try.

BELTANE LOVE SPELL

One afternoon, I decided to call the famous Celtic bard Taliesin. I wanted to hear his voice and know exactly what a real love spell was from ancient times. I lay down on my bed, went into alpha, and meditated on Taliesin. In the middle of the meditation I felt myself sinking into the mattress. I felt as though I was falling deeply asleep. I began to hear music, sweet enchanting music, and a man's voice singing. His voice became clearer and I could see him gazing into my eyes. I knew he was using glamoric (enchantment) and I was the target of his spell. His words caressed me and I felt joy and passion. Suddenly I realized: *This is the bard! This is the spell! I must awake and write this down!* I struggled to get awake. He sang on. I knew I would not remember it all. I finally pulled myself up from the bed and found a pen and paper. This is the spell Taliesin sang to me. You can use this in a love spell of your own, or to feel loved by the God Taliesin:

I am the soft breeze that moves your golden hair.
I am the cool wind that brings color to your face.
I am the spindle that weaves the clothes you wear.
I am the fingers that sew the trim of lace
that crown your beauty,
that warm your heart.
I am the songbird that sings your love,
that sounds your beauty,
that beats your heart.
I am the moonlight that showers your sleep,
that deepens your beauty,
that rests your heart.
I am the starlight that illumines your dreams.
Love is all that it seems.

CLEAN AIR SPELL

You will need:

1 black candle
1 white candle
1 bowl of earth
1 bowl of water
1 thurible with hot coals

3 bird feathers or more (can be chicken, turkey, bluejay, crow—any feather)
parchment paper
1 blue pen
3 yards white cord
3 yards black cord
3 yards blue cord
Rhiannon Oil (see p. 151)
Dana Oil (see p. 151)
1 wand

Cast your Circle. Light charcoals and let them burn without incense. Place the black candle to the left and the white candle to the right. Place the bowl of earth to the North, your thurible to the East, feathers to the South, and water to the West. Anoint the candles with Rhiannon Oil and Dana Oil, then light them and say:

O! mighty Rhiannon, you have carried burdens and have been able to overcome obstacles with faith. Grant us this flame of faith. Give us the strength and wisdom to balance the elements. Dana, Mother of us all, help us to clean this Earth, to balance all elements of the cosmos. So mote it be.

Hold your wand, point it North, and say: *I cleanse, I worship. I am the caretaker of Earth.* Point to the East and say: *I cleanse, I worship. I am the keeper of the Fire.* Point to the South and say: *I cleanse, I worship. I am the breather of Air.* Point to the West and say: *I cleanse, I worship. I am the drinker of Water.*

Pick up your cords, tie a loop at the top, and braid them. While you braid, say or chant:

With whispering wind, my spirit sings. With gusting wind, my spirit moves. With howling winds, my spirit wings to Avalon.

After you have finished the chant, tie a knot in the cord. Continue braiding and chanting until there is only enough room left to tie three knots in succession, leaving three tails of cord hanging free. Pick up some feathers, touch them with your wand and a tiny dab of both Goddess oils. Say:

We ask the Goddesses Dana and Rhiannon to use their might to balance the elements and to cleanse our air. So mote it be.

Take each feather you feel is a powerful totem and stick it into your cords through the braids and knots. On parchment, write with a blue pen:

"I ask this spell to cleanse the air on Earth, so that all the plants, animals, and humans may have fresh clean air forever. So mote it be."

Roll up your parchment and tie it to your cord. Touch the cord and feathers with your wand.

Point the wand to the North and say: *I release the element of Earth to cleanse the Air.* Point to the West: *I release the element of Water to cleanse the Air.* Point to the South: *I release the element of Air to cleanse the Air.* Point to the East: *I release the element of Fire to cleanse the Air.*

Your circle is released. Hang your cord at home, or outdoors if you wish.

BELTANE HEALING SPELL

You will need:

- *parchment*
- *red pen*
- *Bel's Incense (see p. 151)*
- *Dana Oil (see p. 151)*
- *Rhiannon Oil (see p. 151)*
- *sword or blade*
- *charcoal and thurible*

Cast your circle with sword or blade. Light charcoal and place Bel's Incense upon it. Touch the parchment with Dana and Rhiannon oils and write this spell with a red pen:

"I ask this of the Goddess and God of Beltane that health will come instead of pain and suffering; happiness, self-esteem, and a healthy body will maintain forever. I ask this to be correct and for the good of all. So mote it be."

Fold your spell and pass it over the smoke of incense. Release your circle. Take your spell to the person you wish to heal or keep it near you at all times.

HOLIDAY FARE

May is the time of fertility and new beginnings. After a long Winter, everyone feels the warm rumblings of Spring, the deep need to regenerate. The Faeries are afoot. They dance in the hills and roll in the grass, reveling in the joy of a warm May breeze. Our spirits are high with the lust and heartiness of Spring. New life is stirring and appetites are keen.

On Beltane, I often begin my day with a delicious bowl of Irish oatmeal. Oatmeal brings good fortune and encourages the power and magic of the Faeries. I highly recommend a brand called John McCann's Irish Oatmeal, which is available in the United States in Irish shops. Irish oatmeal takes a little longer to prepare, but it is well worth the effort. Served with cream and brown sugar or country butter, Irish oatmeal promises your day will be fruitful and successful.

By Beltane, Mother Earth's bounty has been bestowed upon us once more and we celebrate the land's beautiful array of colors, aromas, and tastes. Spring flowers adorn the table at every meal. Red, white, and green flowers each have special meaning. Red symbolizes love, white sends out energy, and green represents the life force in nature. Daffodils and primroses, strawberry flowers and poppies, encourage and sustain the Faeries' magic and the power of love. This is the time of year we yearn to create life and energy anew. Many revelers dress in red for the Beltane feast, because red is the color of love and marriage, awakening and blossoming.

On Beltane, Witches often use coals from the ritual's Bel fire to give Faerie magic to the holiday meal. We often cook with the budding petals of herbs. Nettle is especially common at Beltane festivities. If you are ever stung by nettle, the ancients say you've been stung by love, and sometimes marriage. On Beltane, children will chase each other in fun with baskets of nettle, teasing each other with the prospects of "love." I was once pricked on my ankle by nettle that grew along the pathway to a gentleman's thatched cottage in England, and, yes, I fell in love with the person who lived there!

Here are some suggestions on what to serve at Beltane, but let your imagination, as well as your emotions, run free.

FEAST OF BELTANE

May Wine
Nettle Soup
Roast Duckling in Orange Sauce
Broccoli and Cauliflower with Cheese Sauce
Green Gooseberry and Elder Flower Compote

MAY WINE

12 sprigs sweet woodruff
1¼ cups confectioner's sugar
1 bottle dry white wine
1 block ice
3 bottles dry white wine
1 qt. soda water or carbonated water, or champagne
spring flowers

Combine woodruff, sugar, and 1 bottle of dry white wine in a large bowl, and cover. After half an hour remove the woodruff. Stir and pour over a block of ice in a large cauldron. Add 3 bottles of wine and the soda water or champagne. Decorate around cauldron base with flowers and ferns.

NETTLE SOUP

1½ oz. butter
1 lb. potatoes, chopped
2 large onions, chopped
6 leeks, chopped
salt and freshly ground pepper to taste
4½ cups chicken stock
5 oz. nettle, washed and chopped (or approx. 2 oz. dried)
¾ cup cream

Melt butter in a deep frying pan or saucepan. When butter foams, add potatoes, onions, and leeks. Stir until coated in butter, then sprinkle with salt and pepper and cover. Cook on low heat for 10 minutes, or until vegetables are soft. Add stock and simmer vegetables. Add nettle leaves and continue to simmer until soft. Do not overcook. Add cream a little at a time. If desired, add more seasonings, such as mint or rosemary or herbed butter. Serves 6.

ROAST DUCKLING IN ORANGE SAUCE

3 large oranges (preferably organically grown)
2 ducklings
1 thin slice lemon, peeled
salt and pepper

FOR THE SAUCE:

grated rind and juice of 2 oranges
2 cups chicken stock
2 tsp. corn flour

Peel oranges and divide into sections. Stuff sections into body cavities of ducklings along with lemon. Place on a rack in a roasting pan. Cook for 30 minutes at 375° F. Remove from oven. Prick skin all over with toothpick and return to the oven for another 30 minutes or until juices run clear when you skewer the skin. Remove ducklings. Scoop out oranges and lemon and discard. Strain fat from roasting pan. In a saucepan, combine rind and stock and bring to a boil. Lower heat and simmer. With a whisk, blend corn flour and orange juice and pour into saucepan. Cook over gentle heat until sauce has thickened and cleared. Brush sauce over breasts of ducklings. Garnish with fresh oranges. Serve sauce separately. *Note:* Cherries may be used instead of oranges, if you wish.

BROCCOLI AND CAULIFLOWER WITH CHEESE SAUCE

2 large heads broccoli
2 large heads cauliflower

Steam and set aside.

FOR THE SAUCE:

1 cup heavy cream
2–3 tbs. water
½ lb. butter
2 large cloves garlic, chopped fine
1 tsp. garlic powder
2 lbs. American cheese, sliced thin
3 tbs. corn flour or flour and water paste (thickener)

Place cream and water in a saucepan, stirring constantly on low heat. Add butter, garlic, and garlic powder. Then add cheese slice by slice, always stirring. After all cheese is melted, add corn flour to thicken. Stir until desired consistency and set aside.

Break up broccoli and cauliflower into florets. Strain well and cool almost to room temperature. Pour warm sauce over vegetables when ready to serve.

GREEN GOOSEBERRY AND ELDER FLOWER COMPOTE

2–3 elder flower heads
2 lbs. green gooseberries (remove tips)
2 cups sugar
2½ cups cold water

Tie elder flowers in a square of unbleached muslin or cotton and place in an enamel saucepan. Add gooseberries, sugar, and water. Bring to a slow boil and boil for 2 minutes or until gooseberries burst. Remove elder flowers. Allow to cool. Serve in a pretty bowl or glass dish and garnish with fresh elder flowers.

ANCIENT ACTIVITIES

In ancient times, warfare was most likely to be conducted from Beltane to Samhain. During the colder months, everyone stayed indoors. On festival days, however, no weapons were raised. Beltane was a sacred time for peace and communion with the Goddesses and Gods. Tribes gathered together for the latest gossip, feasting, and fun. Competitions and games, love and romance were the order of the day.

Today, as in ancient times, Spring brings a renewed and vigorous energy along with a carefree feeling of possibilities. What more important activity could there be in Spring than reveling in the beauty of the season? Drink in the air and blue skies, and enjoy the music of Nature. Birds, crickets, and frogs raise their voices in song. Spring is a time to dance and run about, and to raise our own voices in praise for our planet, Mother Earth.

Go A-Maying Picnic for Two

Nothing is more romantic or fun than a Beltane picnic for two. As the old saying goes, "Hooray! Hooray! It's the first of May, outdoor lovemaking begins today!"

I've included a recipe for May Wine (see p. 158), which would have to be prepared ahead of time. If you don't feel like bothering, simply bring a bottle of wine, or champagne, if you prefer. The herb damiana is an aphrodisiac. Add damiana liqueur to your wine, or you can purchase damiana liqueur in a liquor store. If your eyes are already starry with love, and you do not want to use alcohol, simply mix damiana and honey in a tea. For your outing bring a large blanket big enough for a king-size bed, and two pillows. You may also want to bring your own flowers, a packet of birdseed for the birds, and a natural bug repellent. To keep the bees and ants away, bring a jar of honey and place it at the base of a tree a short distance away from your blanket. If you bring fresh fruit in your basket, plant the seeds so a pear or peach tree might grow. If you don't want to plant seeds, however, remember to bring a package of condoms! (although there are couples who may not need them).

On a go-a-Maying picnic, it is worth the effort to bring serving plates and eating utensils that cannot be discarded. For example, bring cloth napkins, not paper, china plates and real silverware, not plastic, and glass goblets or wine glasses, instead of paper cups. Inexpensive plates and silverware, can always be found at yard sales if your own dishes are too special to use outdoors. Remember, on a picnic, table settings don't have to match. The point is that everything you bring should be able to be brought home with you and washed. This way you don't pollute the environment with anything. Your lovemaking can only bring joy to the environment.

Here are some suggestions for what to bring in your basket:

bottle of damiana-
  infused
  wine or champagne,
  or tea
cheddar cheese
bread

wheat crackers
strawberry spread
tabouli
fresh fruit or fruit salad
flowers and vase
packet of birdseed
jar of honey
natural bug repellent

FLOWER WREATH

Salem Witches spend May Eve making a wreath to hang atop the maypole. On a wreath frame or sturdy natural base, we entwine the beautiful blossoms of new Spring flowers and herbs that grow in our area. To this we add long ribbons of lavenders, pinks, greens, and golds. The flower wreath is suspended around the maypole with four ribbons.

THE MAYPOLE DANCE

The traditional maypole is an oak tree. However, here in New England we often use birch trees. A group of coveners selects a tree and the appropriate thanks and gifts are given in exchange. We ask the tree's permission and then leave tokens of fresh herbs or crystals. We use the same tree year in and year out. Our maypole winters over in my basement. The branches are trimmed, and when Beltane arrives, the tree is secured in a stand. We cover the stand with moss and ferns and flowers and decorate the pole, wrapping it in Springtime ribbons. Our flower wreath is suspended from the top. The maypole can be brought inside as well. The children are all dressed in green and ready to dance and sing:

Maiden May, heal the Earth,
Make this day one of mirth.

Maiden May, heal the Earth,
We return from death to birth.

If you can't make a maypole because you don't have the space or facilities, you can make a miniature one from either an oak or birch branch. You may even use a dowel. Paint it and decorate it with ribbons and flower petals or bake a cake with a maypole decoration, using fresh flower petals and a pencil wrapped in ribbons.

Faery Magic

Children are an especially important part of the Beltane celebration, for what is Springtime but the sensation of feeling young again? In our youth we possess a unique wisdom that is often on par with the gifts of the Faeries. Children often communicate in Faery language, as do animals, knowing and sensing things that we as adults rarely grasp.

Beltane is a favorable time of year for communicating with the Faeries. The powers of the Faeries are particularly strong in May. During this time of year, they are most likely to be espied, though usually out of the corners of your eyes or on the periphery of your vision. Like children, the Faeries love the fresh Spring breezes, the greening Earth, and aroma of blooming flowers. Here is a spell children can do to build self-confidence and protection during Spring.

BELTANE CHILDREN'S SPELL FOR PROTECTION

You will need:

3 tbs. blessed thistle
3 tbs. broom
1 bowl
2 six-inch squares of pink satin or 2 pink magic bags

Faery Fire Oil (see p. 96)
Dana Oil (see p. 151)
Rhiannon Oil (see p. 151)
3 pink cords, each 3 yards long
1 magic wand
1 loved teddy bear
1 pink ribbon, 13 inches long
flowers in bloom
1 vase

Cast your circle with your wand and say:

Circle left, circle right,
like the wheel of colors bright.

Put teddy bear, cords, ribbons, and magic bags in front of you. Make sure herbs and oils are within reach. Put herbs in bowl and drop a few drops of all oils onto herbs. Touch herbs with wand and say:

Faeries protect me.

Put flowers in a nice spot on the altar. Hold the pink cords all together and tie loop at top. Braid together, and as you braid, say or chant:

Mother Dana and Rhiannon,
Faeries protect me.

At the bottom tie three knots. Put herbs in two pink bags. Take the 13-inch ribbon and place it around the neck of your teddy and tie one magic bag to it. Take the second bag full of enchanted herbs and tie to your Celtic knotwork cord. Pick up your teddy and hug him. He represents the god Bel. Release your circle. Hang your cord in your sleeping space and keep your teddy with you when you can. Always do things that are correct and safe. Listen to your parents about what is safe for you and remember that the *sidhe* (or Faeries) will give you wisdom to protect yourself.

MIDSUMMER
Summer Solstice (around June 21st)

Poised in perfect symmetry, the Sun at Midsummer reaches that moment in His journey across the sky when His power peaks and in one magical instant begins to wane. Of course, to many of us, the weakening of the Sun's fiery strength is barely discernible in the hot, dry month of June, but to the ancient Celts, in tune as they were with the ryhthms of Nature, the Sun's sea change was a significant event.

Midsummer shares many of the same bawdy, carefree qualities of Beltane. In his comedy *A Midsummer Night's Dream,* William Shakespeare speaks to the holiday's reputation with a great understanding of Celtic customs and beliefs. As if braiding a Celtic knot, he weaves three separate themes—a wedding, a love story, and an Otherworldly spat—into one unified whole. Amid Midsummer's love "madness," he ultimately brings into balance the activities of the Faery world with our own. Displaying an intimate knowledge of folk story and the absurdities and inconsistencies of humankind, Shakespeare unfolds this frolicking, foolhardy romp in the woods, never once admonishing or instructing his players. As the Faery, Puck, observes, "Lord, what fools these mortals be!" Puck enjoys not only humans but also the differences between his world and ours.

Like the ancient Celts, Shakespeare knew the profound effect Nature, especially the nature of love, has on humanity. When we are in love, we make mistakes. We say and do ridiculous things. But it's Midsummer! We are human and we are in love. In his wisdom, Shakespeare put his trust in Nature and the Wheel of the Year, knowing that as we pass through this enchanted time, all things aright themselves anew.

As we have seen at Winter Solstice, the Oak King, God of the Waxing Year, vanquishes the Holly King, God of the Waning Year. At Midsummer, the reverse is true, with the Holly King wresting the baton from his rival twin. In Celtic mythology, Midsummer is the time of year when the Young God retreats to the ever-turning Wheel of the Stars. These are the enchanted realms of the Goddess Arianrhod, where the God must wait and learn before being born again at Winter Solstice. *Arianrhod* means "silver wheel," and Her palace, known as Caer Arianrhod, is the aurora borealis. She is Goddess of the astral skies, and there She rules over the God's temporary refuge of death as Goddess of Reincarnation. Though Her way is frought with difficulties, as we say in the Craft: "One must suffer to learn." She possesses great wisdom and hidden mysteries, which only those who have been tested can comprehend. The wonderful Celtic bard Taliesin, after undergoing certain periods of life study, finally entered Arianrhod's castle to learn the secrets of death.

ALWAYS, ALWAYS QUESTION AUTHORITY

I always tell my students how important it is to know for themselves and not simply to believe. Don't believe me. Find out for yourself. Read, read, read! But while you do so, always ask yourself who is writing what you read. Who is benefiting when you believe this information? For example, Julius Caesar wrote about the ancient Celtic tribes. What little we learn from him must be taken with much less than a grain of salt and understood within the context of Roman propaganda. While Caesar was writing about the Celts, he was also busy trying to exterminate them. Because Witches have been persecuted for so long, it is difficult to know for sure about many parts of our history. Like many oppressed peoples, we had to go underground and devise secret ways of practicing our beliefs. Much emphasis is put on our bardic tradition, and thank the Goddess we have that! But we also had an alphabet and we had a written history. St. Patrick is responsible for the wide-scale burning of Celtic texts. Even today, just about everything we read about the Celts has a Christian gloss. It is shocking to me to read books by Celtic scholars and historians that nowhere mention the word Witch. They always say Druid. What seems to escape them is that the Druids were Witches. What they practiced was Witchcraft!

EARTH MAGIC

Though Midsummer marks the onset of the Sun's dying strength, the season itself is one of abundance. Flowers and herbs are in full bloom, the days are long, and the nights hot and dry. While the goings-on at Beltane have a playful sense of carefree abandon about them, the hot Midsummer season tends to create in us a fiery, more breathless passion. Couples who have decided to make a go of it at Beltane are still in those heady early days of their relationships. Those who have been together for a year and a day and who decide to continue on in their love for each other are often married in a more formal handfasting at Midsummer or Lughnasadh.

Midsummer is ruled by the Mead Moon, which is also sometimes referred to as the Honey Moon. Many of today's modern wedding traditions hail from pagan origins. Wedding bands are symbols of the Witch's Magic Circle. Tossing the garter and bouquet are also believed to be pagan customs. As Shakespeare's Faery King Oberon says, "Now, until the break of day,/Through this house each Faery stray./ To the best bride-bed will we,/Which by us shall blessed be." The traditional notion that Midsummer is a favorable time of year to get married is clearly an idea begun by the Faeries.

Midsummer is an erotic, sexy time of year, as the Sun blazes hot upon us in full flower and the Summer skies collide with flashes of heat lightning and thunderclouds. It is not surprising that the element of fire is an important part of the Midsummer festivities. The tradition of hurling fire wheels into the air or down from atop a sacred hill was a common practice throughout Europe up until the nineteenth century or even later. A Midsummer fire is traditionally kindled from the friction of two sacred woods, fir and oak. In ancient times, as at Beltane, animal herds were driven between the embers of Midsummer fires to purge them of disease or illness. In some regions, the ashes were rubbed on their hides as a talisman for protection. We also use the ashes from the spells we burn at Beltane to rub on our foreheads to heighten our magical powers. At Beltane, nine sacred woods are used to kindle the Bel fire, but at Midsummer, nine different kinds of herbs are customarily thrown upon the blaze. These herbs can be chosen from the list on pp. 178–9, but mistletoe, vervain, Saint-John's-wort, heartsease, and lavender are usually among the nine chosen.

Flowers are essential to Midsummer's rite. During this time of year I often call upon the Faery Queen and Flower Goddess Vivian. She is Merlin the Magician's wise teacher, and like Blodeuwedd, whom we met at the Spring Equinox, was created in the Otherworld completely from flowers. It is Vivian who gives the sword Excalibur to King Arthur. At Midsummer's ritual, flowers of all kinds and colors are brought to the altar and feast in Vivian's honor.

On Midsummer's Day, we sometimes hold our temple's rite in the backyard of a friend's house. Her yard looks much like a meadow trailing into the woods. Before the late afternoon ritual, we send groups into the woods to collect wildflowers to decorate the edges of the yard. We put these colorful arrays in large jars and buckets of water and then place them among the weeds or shrubs, giving the yard the appearance of a Summer field in bloom. Early in the morning everyone gathers before the first burst of light. We face East and wait to shower in the brilliance of the Sun's strongest rays. We hold sacred power tools, such as crystals, blades, and swords to be used later in the ritual, to absorb the Sun's energy.

As the day goes on, more coveners arrive carrying armfuls of magical tools, food, and flowers. Many of us set to the enjoyable task of adorning our hair. A few of us have become quite good at making flower wreaths and help others to learn. Children always love the Summer outdoor festivals, because these give them a chance to wear their Faery wings and to dance and sing the Witch songs they have learned.

If I don't choose to meet with the others at daybreak on Midsummer's Day, I rise at dawn to spend the morning enjoying my herb and flower garden. The Flower Faeries are powerful at this time. I light votive candles on my garden altar and often leave Faery gifts, like cookies or cakes or fruit for the animals. I fill a chalice with spring water and cover it with a saucer to prevent wasps or ladybugs from drinking it. I will bring this chalice inside to use in my magic for the day, either to attract Faery power or to heighten my psychic ability and energy. In the morning and later on after the ritual in the evening, I light stick incense that is easy to put in the ground. As the Sun rises higher, all the colors brighten in the garden and butterflies and birds begin to spread their wings and sing. I always thank the herbs and leave a gift for the Faeries before cutting them. I always cut flowers and herbs on Midsummer Day in a ritual manner with my hand sickle. These I will use for wreaths in my hair in preparation for the large gathering in the afternoon.

Preparations

Summer flowers with golden yellow, scarlet red, white, pink, and violet blooms decorate the Midsummer altar. In addition to the traditional black, white, and red candles representing the Triple Goddess, I use a yellow-gold candle to represent the Sun. The altar cloth is usually black or gold and I usually have a fresh sprig of oak and holly to represent the Oak and Holly kings. For the following ritual you will need a silver ring for the High Priestess, as well as all the oils mentioned in this chapter.

What to Wear

The High Priestess usually wears her traditional black robes or may also wear white, gold, beige, green, red, or brown. Priests each wear crowns of half oak and half holly. You may want to wear a gold torque, or a Celtic knotwork pin. Some of us wear our tartans to represent a family's heritage. Chain mail is making a comeback in today's fashion. You might want to wear a gauntlet or chain-mail vestment. Again, wear as much makeup and jewelry as you desire. The Celts were not modest in their dress.

The Ritual

Cast your Circle.

The High Priestess faces North with her peyton in her left hand. She says: *I call the Great Boar. His Earth-bound body is a spirit's dwelling.* She faces East and says: *I call the Dragon. His great body breathes fire creating the mist of spirit.* She faces South and says: *I call the Raven. The spirit of air lifts her mighty ebony wings.* She faces West and says: *I call the Mermaid. Her song creates the Ninth Wave.*

The High Priest and High Priestess anoint the candles with Merlin Oil and Arianrhod Oil (see pp. 181–2) and light them.

High Priestess and High Priest: *Silver ring of steadfastness, O! Goddess that carries our burdens for us, come to this flame. Dragon's mist and standing stone, that proves magic again and again, O! mighty Merlin, speak to us in this flame.*

The High Priestess takes her wand and makes three circles above her head clockwise.

High Priestess: *The triple spiral is my path.*

The High Priest takes his wand and anoints it with Dragon's Mist Oil (see p. 182). He makes two circles above his head.

High Priest: *The two dragons are my path.*

The High Priestess holds the chalice for the world to see and walks in a circle.

High Priestess: *The waters of life harbor the ring of stars.*

The High Priest holds his blade to the sky and turns in a circle.

High Priest: *The two dragons lie in a circle at our feet.*

The High Priest places the blade in the cup.

High Priest: *Star fire, strike this blade. This is the light from which Excalibur was made. As the sun rises through the standing stones in our holy land, we envision its rays rising from the chalice.*

The High Priestess once again raises the chalice for all to see.

High Priestess: *Light of our beginnings, God, Goddess, balance once more this world in which we live. Help us to see the doorway between the worlds and exist in both. Sunrise marks the time of dreams come true, beyond the power of us all is the power of the dragons.*

High Priest: *We come from a time before dark and our protection comes from beyond the power of us all.*

High Priestess: *The sword of light protects women who are both Faery and human.*

High Priest: *The sword of light protects men who are both Faery and human.*

High Priestess: *Vivian, Goddess of the* sidhe, *Vivian will wear the silver ring of Arianrhod, and the power of women will be doubled.*

High Priest: *The Merlin shall pour dragon's blood into our veins, and the power of men shall be doubled.*

Both High Priest and High Priestess hold their hands up, palms to the rising sun.

High Priest and High Priestess: *My hands blaze with the power of the fiery Sun. Great God, be with us always. So mote it be.*

All raise hands and repeat: *My hands blaze with the*

power of the fiery Sun. Great God, be with us always. So mote it be.

High Priestess: *We ask the mighty Sun to bless the Earth, replenish our rain forests, and the ancient forests shall return. Bless the Mother Earth with the seed of life always. So mote it be.*

High Priest and High Priestess: *We are the Faery blood of your beginnings. We are your children. Guide us to heal the Earth, Air, Sky, and Water. So mote it be.*

The High Priest pours water from the chalice into the cauldron.

High Priestess: *I breathe the magic of my makers into this cauldron.*

The High Priestess blows upon the water. The High Priest puts his finger in the water and places it to his lips, then places his finger on the silver ring on the altar. He picks up the ring.

High Priest: *Silver stardust come to rest in this world.*

The High Priest places the ring on Vivian's (the High Priestess's) finger.

High Priestess: *Firelight and steamy mists climb to this world. So mote it be.*

All in circle are touched with Faery Flower Oil, especially on their forehead and on the flowers they wear in their hair.

The High Priest faces North with the peyton and says: *Farewell, Great Boar, blessed is your great spirit.* He faces West and says: *Farewell, Mermaid, blessed is your song that sets the motion of the Ninth Wave.* He faces South and says: *Farewell, Raven, blessed are your mighty wings.* He faces East and says: *Farewell, Great Dragon, blessed is the fire you breathe.*

This releases the circle.

Magical Herbs

Midsummer is the season of fresh, magically potent herbs. By this time of year an herb's magical energy is gleaned not from its roots, as in Wintertime, but from its buds, flowers, leaves, and stems. Now many herbs are ready to be gathered for savory dishes and Summertime drinks. Culinary herbs like basil, mint, sage, fennel, chives, and rosemary are venerable and well-deserved favorites in anyone's kitchen. Midsummer is also the time to begin drying herbs (see p. 212). Two herbs sacred to the ancient Celts are ritually gathered during this time of year. Vervain is always picked Midsummer morning with your left hand. Mistletoe, which has yet to bear its berries by Midsummer, is harvested at the exact moment of Summer Solstice and used for protection. By Winter this vibrant evergreen bears its berried fruit and is used for fertility. The herb must be cut with a charged golden (or bronze, actually) sickle and let to fall upon white silk or linen, never touching the ground. As Sir James Frazier writes in *The Golden Bough,* mistletoe was considered "the seat of life" for the oak. As long as mistletoe curled about the oak's trunk, as it is wont to do, the oak would never die.

Following is a list of the more popular Midsummer herbs and flowers:

sage	rosemary
mint	thyme
basil	hyssop
fennel	honeysuckle
chive	red heather
chervil	white heather
tarragon	rue
parsley	sunflower

lavender
fern
mistletoe
Saint-John's-wort
mugwort
vervain
meadowsweet
heartsease
feverfew
iris
rowan
oak
fir
pine
aniseed
hazelnut

Philtres, Incense, and Oils

Midsummer is often a good time of year to seek protection and to purify space against negative or harmful energy. Witches make philtres to use with talismans of protection for home, pets, and wild animals. Rowan branches hung over doorways or over barns and outbuildings keep them safe from unwanted intruders. Rue is used for healing and protecting against disease. The enchanting scent of lavender is an ideal ingredient for a Midsummer incense. This is also the season we look ahead for answers about fertility and love. Certain Midsummer oils can be worn or used in spells to divine the future marriage prospects of young women and men. It is said that in ancient times on Midsummer's Eve, young women galloped through the fields of growing crops on broomsticks to ensure a bountiful harvest and encourage personal fertility as well. From this agricultural ritual, Christians created the evil image of the flying Witch on a broomstick so sadly ingrained on our modern-day psyches.

Here are a few samples to spark your own imaginative blends:

MIDSUMMER PHILTRE

heather
fennel seed
corn
wheat
hyssop
feverfew
fir
pine
Saint-Joan's-wort
3 drops Faery Flower Oil (see p. 181)

Mix all ingredients together and bind with a few drops of Faery Flower Oil. Place in a bowl on a table or in a jar or magic bag to be carried with you.

SUMMER SOLSTICE INCENSE

Blend equal parts of the following:

heather
oak leaves
rosemary
wheat or crushed corn
sunflower leaves
vervain
3 drops Mermaid Oil (See below.)

Combine all ingredients and keep in a magic bottle or bowl or magic bag.

MERMAID OIL

The Mermaid is a part of my magical Celtic heritage. My name, Laurie, comes from the McLaren tribe of Scotland. One of that family's ancient symbols is the Mermaid. I personally use the twin-tailed Mermaid in much of my magic, because I am a Pisces and part Scot. Here is my own personal recipe for Mermaid Oil:

2 drams hazelnut oil
pinch seaweed
1 pebble
1 seashell
pinch sea salt

Warm all ingredients in an enamel pan. Let cool. Pour into tiny bottles or jars and use to anoint candles and in spells.

FAERY FLOWER OIL

1 dram elder oil
a few dried rosebuds
1 dram lavender oil

Warm slowly in an enamel saucepan. Let cool. Pour into magic bottles and use in spellwork, philtres, and ritual anointing.

MERLIN OIL

1 dram hazelnut oil
1 dram fir oil
*1 pebble from Tinthele (the crystal cave where Merlin sleeps)**
*1 sprig sacred oak from England that has been struck by lightning**

* These must be purchased at a Witch supply store, but you may also substitute a pebble indigenous to your area. If you can't find an oak that has been struck by lightning, use any oak sprig, realizing, however, that its energy is not nearly as powerful as one struck by lightning.

ARIANRHOD OIL

1 dram cedar oil
1 dram grape oil
1 dram honeysuckle oil
1 silver star (glitter stars)

Gently warm over low flame in an enamel pan. Remove from heat and let cool. Store in clear jars or magic bottles.

DRAGON'S MIST OIL

1 sprig broom, cut fine
1 piece Irish moss, cut fine
2 pinches vervain
½ tsp. sea salt
1 dram heather oil
1 dram oak moss
3 drams witch hazel
1 dram pine oil

Blend in an enamel saucepan on very low heat. Let cool and place in small bottle or jar with lid.

Magical Stones

Stones sing with the echoes of Earth's beginnings. Witches know that stones are magical objects. Each one is the herald of a marvel, an embodiment of the eternal verity of the cosmos. There is no presence so weighty nor so powerful an enchanter as stone. Like the prophet Merlin, who sleeps in the crystal cave, stones are creations beautiful and strange, the standard-bearers of auspicious signs of Nature. I often wonder what went into their making. What alchemy of history and Otherworldly genius created them? At Midsummer, the shortest night of the year, we see the stars rise with a grateful sense of familiarity but also with an uncertain yearning to know their secrets. What are stars but celestial stones? What convulsions of Nature have brought them here to the surface for our benefit and use? Perhaps only Merlin knows the answer to these, Arianrhod's gifts.

The Midsummer stone landscape is ablaze with the fire of the Sun and the liquid, clear sounds of the element of Water. We use stones in philtres or wear them as jewelry and amulets to attract love and light and to keep us healthy and safe from harm. Following is a list of some of Midsummer's more telling stones:

ruby
garnet
diamond
seashell
Herkimer diamond
clear quartz crystal
amber
citrine
cat's-eye
yellow topaz
yellow tourmaline
gold
silver

Magical Spells

The Great Sorcerer, Merlin, possesses an array of psychic abilities that can be invoked around this time of year for promoting protection, counseling, and scrying into the future. Hailing from both the Welsh and the British traditions, Merlin is also named Merddin and Myrddin. Having acquired his knowledge of the ways of enchantment from the Goddess Vivian, Merlin is seer, poet, shapeshifter, master of illusion, wise Witch, and prophet. He dwells in the spirit of the sacred oak, but sleeps in the crystal cave where he harbors the powerful dragon spirit. His magical garments are like the midnight sky sprinkled with stars and planets, and he speaks his magic through the power in the standing stones. According to legend, Merlin built Stonehenge.

In Salem, and in much of the northeastern United States, there are no ancient woods. But in western Massachusetts, near Lenox, there still exist deep woods with gnarly trees and cool springs that pop out seemingly from nowhere. This is a place where I especially feel the spirit of Merlin. I often call upon Merlin at Midsummer to aid me in spellwork and meditation. I own several magical items from where Merlin once tread, and I have been handed down items that have been touched by his power. I write down short poems or lines that come to me while I try to envision his presence and enchanted surroundings. Here is an example of a short poem I wrote about Merlin's dragon spirit that helped me to better focus upon my magic. It is from the liturgy of the Cabot tradition.

THE DRAGON'S MIST

Wind among the boughs did song,
and the dragon's wings did move
across the Midnight sky.
Trails of mist on Earth so long,
and the dragon's breath did prove,
Merlin did not lie.

Here is another about an enchanted Mermaid. This is a poem inspired during a meditation. A vision came to me of a beautiful seashore overlooking moonlit sparkling aqua-blue waters. Just offshore were a few smooth rocks. I saw a beshelled arm slide across a small rock, and there she was. Half her body was in the water. Her hair floated on the ripples and her arm rested upon the stone. I heard her siren song.

MERMAID SONG

The blue wave feathers white;
her green hair lays spread on the water bright.
Mist, not meant to drink,
sprinkled with starlight falls from the link
of her shelled arm.

As the Sun begins its downward slide, Summer Solstice can also be a time of anxiety about the future. In effect, Midsummer marks the beginning of the end for the beneficent God of the Sun. We seek assurances of a bountiful crop, hope for the health and productivity of animals, and take steps to secure and protect our homes.

Here are two spells to aid you during this paradoxical season of both abundance and concern about what lies ahead:

SPELL OF THE NINTH WAVE

Go to the seashore or a pond to get water. If you have none of these in your area, use a large bowl of water. You will also need:

- *2 light blue and 2 light green candles*
- *9 seashells*
- *1 sea wand (made from driftwood or from sterling silver crystal with shells and blue and green stones)*
- *seaweed*
- *1 empty bowl*
- *1 green glass bottle with top*
- *green string or ribbon*
- *Mermaid Oil (see p. 180)*
- *Summer Solstice Incense (see p. 180)*
- *sea salt*
- *1 lb. sand or dirt from shore*
- *sea glass (You can*

stroll along a beach to collect sea glass or seashells. If you cannot, you can omit sea glass from the spell.)
1 pt. water from pond, ocean, or lake of your choice
amulet or something to symbolize the moon—a silver mermaid, a moonstone, a silver spoon, anything made from silver
amulet or something to symbolize the sun—citrine stone, a gold sunface, or a yellow flower

Anoint the candles with Mermaid Oil and say: *Merrow (mermaids), come to this magic place and bring with you a safe storm, one of protection. Caesa (pronounced* say-sa), *come to these shores and protect our waters from all pollution.*

Light the charcoal and sprinkle Summer Solstice Incense on it. Stand with your hands upward and hold your sea wand. Speak to the nine maidens that guard the hollows. Say: *Your power is restored. The priestesses of the Temple of the Nine Wells hold the golden cups and the wells are guarded from all who would rape and pillage their sweet waters.*

Then speak to the merrow: *Merrow, send the Ninth Wave to protect the waters of the earth.*

Touch your sea wand to the nine shells, the bottle and bowl of water, seaweed, sea salt, sand, and the water from the sea or lake. Pick up the nine shells and put them in the green bottle, add a pinch sea salt and pinch of dirt or sand, a little bit of seaweed, and three drops Mermaid Oil. Feel the bottle and tie the amulets to the bottle. Hold the bottle and say: *I will keep this bottle. Its power will call the mermaids to protect the waters of land and sea.*

Put some of the seaweed, water, salt, sand, Mermaid Oil,

and amulets into the bowl. Place the bowl out-of-doors. If you live in the city, put it on a porch or garden. If you live near the shore, place it on the edge of the shore, where no one will find it, under a rock or in the ocean. Place your green bottle in a window where light from the Sun and Moon sends messages to the Mermaids and the Nine Guardians of the Wells. Once in a while, when you meditate upon this important spell, repeat the poem I wrote or one you write yourself to conjure the image of the mermaids and rekindle the spell.

MERLIN'S MIST SPELL

You will need:

- *Dragon's Mist Oil (see p. 182)*
- *Merlin Oil (see p. 181)*
- *1 piece parchment*
- *1 red pen*
- *2 green, 2 red, 1 black, and 1 white candle*
- *1 large stone to place in a sacred site, such as your own outdoor shrine, circle, or garden. If you have none of those, then find a place outdoors to place the stone where Earth needs power to survive.*
- *Midsummer Philtre (see p. 180)*
- *Summer Solstice Incense (see p. 180)*
- *thurible, charcoal, and matches*
- *1 wand*
- *1 sword*
- *1 crystal ball*
- *1 small cauldron*

Place the two green and two red candles on each side of the altar. Place black on the left and white on right. Anoint the green and red candles with Dragon's Mist Oil while saying: *O! mighty dragons, fly here in this sacred space, bring with you the fire of making.*

Anoint the black and white candles with Merlin Oil. Touch the black one and say: *Merlin, God of the Standing Stones, you bring to this magic the fire and breath of the dragon.* Touch the white candle and say: *Merlin, maker of magic, send your dragons to the wind to tell the universe of our spell.*

Put your incense on the charcoal, hold your wand, and call Merlin to come into your sacred circle. Touch your wand to the stone and say: *Out of stone, into life, Great Merlin, come into this magical circle with me. I am your servant, your child, I am of the* sidhe. *Come to this place. Let us make a spell together.*

Envision in your mind Merlin standing in front of you and he will come. Hold your sword upright in front of you and swear to the ancient ones: *This sword entrusted to me shall be used to protect the Earth from any who would come to do her harm. I swear by my life and my power in the sight of Merlin that I shall do all in my power to protect the Earth.*

On your parchment write the following spell with a red pen:

"To all who hear me, know this well: the Earth is protected by the dragon's power, the power of Merlin, and by my life. Warning to all who come to do harm, all that you do that is harmful shall be negated and neutralized and all that you have done that is harmful shall be undone and you shall act against Her no more. I ask the God and Goddess that if this spell is not to your liking, it shall not come to be."

HOLIDAY FARE

As Witches, we see the mystical side of a meal. Food is a way to bring people together, and the mouthwatering, thirst-quenching fare of Midsummer provides the perfect opportunity to do just that. This is the season for outdoor dining. Warm Summer nights are best spent on patios and porches appreciating fine food and drink and enjoying the company of close friends and family. In a magically prepared meal, life sweeps in from all directions in wonderful variations. Midsummer's bounty brings us the pure and enduring promise of the land. The power of our magic upon culinary traditions performs important work, as we serve up Midsummer's juicy fruits and vegetables, whole-grain breads, and dishes that use savory fresh herbs instead of dried. As you prepare your Midsummer meal, take care that you use charged herbs and meditate upon the meaning and positive magic of your ingredients.

The menu offered here uses a wide variety of foods. Of course, the more powerful way of eating is to eat regionally, but this is not always possible. Oranges and pineapples are not native to New England, for example, but I do eat them. The point is to try to eat foods from your region as often as possible. The menu prepared below works well outside, but if you happen to get stuck in a surprise Summer thundershower, the meal can easily be moved indoors where equipment and utensils are convenient.

FEAST OF ARIANRHOD

Midsummer Mead
Solstice Herb Bread
Cold Tomato Soup
Grilled Salmon Steaks in Chive Sauce
Starry Fennel Cucumbers in Summer Green Dressing
Any and All Fruit Salad

MIDSUMMER MEAD

1 gal. water	*$2\frac{1}{2}$ lbs. honey*
2 tsp. cinnamon	*12 oz. fruit juice (strawberry or pineapple, your choice)*
1 sprig saffron	*$\frac{1}{2}$ cake yeast*
2 tsp. powdered ginger	
5 whole cloves	
2 capfuls rosewater	

Bring water to a slow boil with cinnamon, saffron, ginger, cloves, and rosewater. Add honey until dissolved, then add fruit juice. Cover tightly and boil for 15 minutes. Cool to lukewarm. Dissolve yeast in warm water and add. Cover with towel for 2 days before straining and bottling. You may need to air mixture periodically. To eliminate the need for airing, a fermentation lock may be purchased from a home-brewing supplies distributor.

SOLSTICE HERB BREAD

3 cups flour	*2 tsp. chopped fresh rosemary*
1 tbs. sugar	*1 tsp. fresh thyme*
1 tsp. salt	*$1\frac{1}{4}$ cups hot water*
1 pkg. dry active yeast	*2 tbs. Crisco*
2 tbs. chopped fresh chives	

Mix 2 cups of the flour, sugar, salt, and yeast in a large bowl. Add herbs, water, and Crisco. Beat slowly, stirring in remaining cup of flour until smooth. Scrape batter from sides of bowl and let rise in a warm place for 35 minutes or until it doubles in bulk. Punch down and beat with a spoon for about 15 seconds. Place dough in a greased loaf pan, patting down and forming loaf shape with your hands. Cover and let rise again for about 30 minutes or until it again doubles in bulk. Bake at 375° F for 40 to 45 minutes. Brush top with butter or margarine and remove from pan to let cool.

COLD TOMATO SOUP

2 large tomatoes, peeled, seeded, and chopped
1 sweet pepper, seeded and chopped
1 clove garlic, peeled and chopped
¾ cup herb blend including basil, chives, tarragon, parsley, dill, chervil, and thyme
½ cup olive oil
3 tbs. lemon juice
3 cups cold water
1 sweet Spanish onion, peeled and sliced
1 cup cucumber, peeled, seeded, and sliced
½ tsp. paprika

Put chopped tomatoes, pepper, garlic, and herbs in a bowl. Stir in olive oil, lemon juice, and cold water. Add onion, cucumber, and paprika. Chill in refrigerator for 5 hours. Serve over ice cubes in bowls and garnish with fresh parsley or watercress.

GRILLED SALMON STEAKS IN CHIVE SAUCE

¾-inch-thick salmon steaks
olive oil or melted butter

FOR THE SAUCE:

2 leeks, chopped fine
fresh chives, chopped
1 bay leaf
pinch peppercorns
2 cups dry white wine
2 tbs. white wine vinegar
½ cup sweet unsalted butter
1 cup heavy cream

To prepare sauce: Bring leeks, chives (leaving some left over to use as garnish), bay leaf, peppercorns, wine, and wine vinegar to a boil in a saucepan. Remove from burner and add butter and cream. Reheat slowly over low heat, keeping it warm before serving.

To prepare salmon: Brush steaks with olive oil or melted butter. Broil or grill for 5 minutes. Baste, turn over, and broil for another 5 minutes or until bone is loose or until pink inside. Serve with warm sauce on side, over steaks, or place steaks on top of sauce and garnish with remaining chives.

STARRY FENNEL CUCUMBERS IN SUMMER GREEN DRESSING

4 cucumbers
¼ cup vegetable oil
2 tbs. lemon juice
1 tsp. fennel seed
½ tsp. salt
¼ cup finely chopped onion

Wash and peel cucumbers. Slice in circles. Cut cucumber slices into star shapes with a star-shaped cookie cutter. Place in Tupperware bowl with lid. Add oil, lemon juice, fennel seed, salt, and onion. Cover and refrigerate for 12 to 15 hours, stirring every so often.

FOR THE DRESSING:

1 cup mayonnaise
¼ cup chives
¼ cup parsley
6 to 8 sprigs fresh dill
2 tsp. tarragon vinegar

Blend on high speed until creamy. Chill for 2 hours and serve on cucumbers.

ANY AND ALL FRUIT SALAD

1 fresh whole pineapple, cut, sliced, and cubed
½ lb. fresh cherries
1 grapefruit, separated into sections
2 mandarin oranges, separated into sections
1 lb. seedless red and green grapes
2 cups green and orange melon balls or wedges
2 peaches, pitted and cubed
2 nectarines, pitted and cubed
½ pt. fresh strawberries
2 plums, cubed

Toss all ingredients in a large fruit bowl. For a dressing, whip until stiff 1 cup heavy cream, 2 tablespoons pineapple juice, and dash salt in chilled bowl.

ANCIENT ACTIVITIES

The Summer months were often times of conflict for the ancient Celtic tribes. After the many mythical intruders from beyond the Ninth Wave, the Celts were also invaded by the Vikings, Romans, Normans, and Anglo-Saxons. From the time of King Edward I, who invited all of the Welsh poets, musicians, and artisans to his castle to massacre them, armies and enemy ideas alike have tried to obliterate a culture that refuses to die. Even today we see the insidious pressures of modern life attempting to kill off what remains of the Celtic tongue—the oldest living languages on Earth—Welsh, Irish Gaelic, Scottish Gaelic, and Manx. The Celts were known, however, for their fierce fighting men and women. The Celtic Warrior Queen Boudicca almost single-handedly wiped out a Roman legion. Today we must continue to fight on both the spiritual and the political fronts to keep our traditions alive.

MAPPING THE CELTIC INFLUENCE

Many of us think of the Celtic influence as affecting only the tribes that hailed from the British Isles. Nothing could be further from the truth. The Celtic tribes were always moving, growing, and changing. Their people engendered the tribes of many other lands. Many of the Greek myths are thought to be of Celtic origin. Celtic customs and traditions are found all across Europe, the Mediterranean, India, Turkey, Asia, and beyond. As we shall see (see pp. 234–5), there is new evidence showing that the Celts traveled far beyond the Ninth Wave to settle in North America long before the Vikings.

June days are so long with sunlight that there is time enough to get many things accomplished and enjoy oneself as well. This is the season for traveling, gardening, and having fun outside. Children play sports and imaginary games in city parks and country fields. We go on hikes in the mountains, nature walks to identify herbs in the wild, or take long walks on the beach. Bike riding, swimming, and camping out under the stars are just a few of the wonderful Summertime activities that bring us the pleasure and generous gifts of the Goddess around this time of year. Here are some ideas on how you can get outside, enjoy Nature, and appreciate the warmth of the Sun before He begins His downward change in course.

GODDESS AND GOD WREATHS

Wreaths can be made to represent any Goddess or God. You can make eight wreaths, one for each holiday. The wreath is a sacred circle representing the Wheel of the Year, the eternal circle of life. An Arianrhod wreath, for example, can be made from Summer flowers and cutout silver stars. Make a Mermaid wreath with seaweed (Irish moss) and shells. Seaweed takes a few days to dry out in the hot Sun. If you don't have seaweed, use tree moss. Use a wire base or form a base with a grape vine and weave the dried seaweed in and out between the frame. Attach seashells or other beach-combing treasures by gluing or tying them to the base with ribbon. Some of us are more clever than others and can manipulate figures out of papier-mâché. If you are handy with this skill, you can make a Merlin wreath by shaping two dragons touching their tails in a circle. Paint it using green, yellow, and red. Add a ruby or garnet to bring it to life. A wreath's magical power can be doubled or tripled depending on how many symbols you choose to use. For example, adding Arianrhod's silver stars to your Mermaid wreath of shells doubles the power of the wreath. Add Summer flowers and you capture the spirit of Vivian, and so on. Use your imagination. It's a gift from the Goddess!

Faery Magic

In *A Midsummer Night's Dream,* Shakespeare's portrayal of the Faeries as powerful, complex, and friendly beings exhibits a deep knowledge of the Otherworld. He never equates them with devils or ghosts, as so many in his time did. The play's language reveals Shakespeare's intimate understanding of the humor, candor, and wisdom kept alive in Faery lore and the Celtic oral tradition. It's as if the Faeries themselves helped him write the play, and I believe Shakespeare, a loyal friend of the Faeries, would be the first to admit it!

Like Beltane, Midsummer is a good time to contact the Faery world. In their wisdom, the Faeries know that Summer Solstice is a moment of fulfillment for Nature. As humans, however, we must often seek an inner path in order to understand the world around us. Meditation and ritual show us the presence of the Faery spirit. The Faery spirit is the great force and energy moving in all things, helping to empower our magic. The Faeries can help us find stones and gems, for example, but we must discern their meaning. Old memories reside just below our conscious field of awareness, so meanings are sometimes temporarily lost or forgotten. My earlier book, *Power of the Witch: The Earth, the Moon, and the Magical Path to Enlightenment,* includes a chart with the meanings of stones, elements, and other information, which makes it easier to find answers to Faery riddles. Midsummer is the time to ask the Faeries for protection and confidence to look into the future while you spend your days outdoors enjoying the Sun. Here are two Faery Garden spells for you to try, one for indoors and one for outdoors:

FAERY GARDEN SPELLS

In some ways a small garden is a way of contributing to the ecological needs of our society. Composting, fertilizing, weeding, and growing flowers, tomatoes, cucumbers, and fresh herbs make me feel that by touching the Earth every day I, too, am nurtured. In this way I feel much more aware of the Earth's seasonal changes. At this moment, while writing these spells for Summer, New England is white with a nor'easter raging. My garden is white and the Snow Queen is reigning. I have just filled all the bird feeders and placed some food out for all the stray cats and dogs. The snowflakes are still in my hair as I sit down to write, so the thoughts of Spring and Summertime are much more precious. Therefore, today I'll be using my crystal garden, looking at my outdoor garden from a safe and warm window.

CRYSTAL FAERY GARDEN SPELL

You'll need:

1 small short-rimmed bowl or flowerpot

3 or more crystals of your liking, such as clear quartz, amethyst, citrine, rose quartz (I prefer the polished natural

crystals and I use more clear quartz than any other in my bowl.)
enough sand to fill a bowl (This you may collect from a beach or from an aquarium store. If you use sand from a beach, I suggest that you put it in a baking pan and place it in the oven at 475° F for 1 hour to make sure any germs or microorganisms are purified.)

Before casting the circle I gather flowers and sacred woods when convenient and a few vegetables to place on my altar. Four to twelve days before you are ready for this spell, cover the crystals with sea salt in a bowl.

You'll also need:

1 yellow, 1 green, 1 red, 1 blue, 1 white, and 1 black votive candle
1 Faery wand
1 thurible
Summer Solstice Incense (see p. 180)
Faery Flower Oil (see p. 181)
Faery Fire Oil (see p. 96)
1 pink, 1 black, and 1 green magic bag
1 large bowl of spring water
1 white towel, new and clean

You'll need to decide what kind of spells you want to put into the crystals. Decide, for example, which one is for love, power, money, protection of family, animals, psychic ability, self-esteem.

Cast your circle with your Faery wand. Anoint candles with Faery Flower Oil, light them, and say: *The fire of Summer comes to this magic space. The sparkle of light from these magic candles shall bring to this magic garden all the power the* sidhe *can give to Earth. So mote it be.*

Light the charcoal, sprinkle with incense, and place the sand in a bowl. Take each crystal one by one out of the salt, wash and dry it, and hold it in the smoke of the incense. Put each crystal to your lips and out loud tell the crystal what you want it to do. Place them in the bowl of sand. Charge your magic bags so that you can take a crystal out of the bowl and carry it with you when you need it.

To bring the Faery Goddesses to your circle and into the bowl, make three circles above your head with the Faery wand. Anoint yourself with Faery Flower Oil and say: *O! Great Goddesses of the* sidhe, *come abide with me. I am your daughter and keeper of your faith. In this sunlit time bring to me your flowering power. Help me to tend myself, to help heal the Earth, and enjoy your great beauty.*

Touch your wand to all crystals, bowl, sand, and magic bags. Sprinkle incense on the charcoal and pass your wand through the smoke and say: *I am grateful for your love and power. I have pride in my Faery faith. This garden is the tool of your powers. So mote it be.*

Release your circle. Place the bowl on the altar or on an end table near where you rest. While meditating you can reach out and hold a crystal and recharge yourself with Faery power.

Faery gardens can be both day- and night-blooming gardens. The night garden looks soft bathed in moonlight with tiny votive candles twinkling, mimicking the night sky. Here is a list of night-blooming flowers to use in your Moon garden:

"Moonlight" cosmos
Centaurea imperialis
baby's breath
white love-in-a-mist
Empress Iberis
sweet rocket
nicotiana
"White Swan" echinacea
moonflower
satin flower
White Cleome
nemophila
"Yellow Goddess" stock
dusky yellow wallflower
night-scented stock
pink evening primrose
cosmos pinkie
"Polar Star" dimorphotheca
"Carpet of Snow" alyssum
"Violet Queen" alyssum
foxglove "Yellow Bells"
aquilegia "The Crystal Star"
Scabiosa "Silver Moon"

OUTDOOR FAERY GARDEN SPELL

Recognizing the Faery power in plants and woodland-type surroundings empowers the Earth from miles around and in the process empowers you and the plants that you will harvest for magical food, incense, potions, and philtres. Many of the plants in my garden are seedlings from seeds that were psychically planted at Samhain, charged at Imbolc, and planted at Beltane. Many of these plants have bloomed for years. I have a national park near my house. The park rangers who do most of the gardening in the area often come to see my garden. They remark at the size and brilliance of my flowers and plants. I always tell them the truth even if they don't believe me. The Faeries tend my garden! For the following spell you will need:

1 Faery wand
1 thurible
Summer Solstice incense (see p. 180)
1 black, 1 white, 1 blue, 1 pink, and 1 green votive candle

Faery Fire Oil (see p. 96)
Faery Flower Oil (see p. 181)
seeds, plants, and cut flowers from the garden
small round top to a wooden table or small round piece of marble (You can buy small tables with screw-on legs in most linen stores and a piece of marble to roll out pastry at a housewares store.)
3 large rocks or crystals to use as legs for this altar top
1 bowl
1 chalice with spring water
1 blue napkin

Cast your circle around your garden far enough to give you room to set up your altar outdoors. Always do a circle on a waxing moon or three days before the full moon. Light all candles, anoint with both Faery oils, and say: *Great Goddess of the* sidhe, *come abide with me. I am your daughter and keeper of your faith. In this sunlit time bring to me your flowering power, your power to do all magic, help me to tend myself, heal the Earth, and enjoy your great beauty. So mote it be.*

Sprinkle incense on the charcoal. Fill the bowl with dirt from the garden. Place the blue napkin over the chalice of water. Point your wand to the North and say: *I call the element of Earth. King Bran, come to this magic garden to empower us.* Point to the South and say: *I call the element of Air. Faery Queen Cerridwen, come to this magic garden as the owl watches this magic day and night.* Point to the East and say: *I call the element of Fire. I call the Faery Queen Maeve, come to this magic garden and strike magic into the color of this flora.* Point to the West and say: *I call the element of*

Water. Merrows, bring your mist to shower magic upon this garden.

Take the napkin from the chalice, hold the chalice toward the garden, and say: *Into this cup I bring all the correct energies of the cosmos and the ancient ones, the Tuatha de Danaan. I call the Goddess of us all, Dana, into this holy water.*

Put your thumb into the water three times and to your lips, tasting the spirit of all you have gathered into the holy water. Take a few drinks from it and pour the rest of it into the bowl of dirt. Touch both hands to the dirt and say: *This is Otherworldly. This is the Faeryland. It belongs to my garden.*

Sprinkle handfuls of the sacred earth all around between the plants or trees and as the sacred dirt touches the ground, your garden is sparked with Faery magic forever.

Release the four elements and release the circle.

LUGHNASADH
(August 1st)

★

The Irish God Lugh is known as the "Bright or Shining One." He is associated with both the Sun and agricultural fertility, since his foster mother died from preparing the lands of Ireland for planting. His festival is in her honor. He is also a God of All Skills and champion of the Tuatha de Danaan or "children of the Goddess Dana." In the Tuatha de Danaan's battle to capture Ireland from the Fomorians, he swaps a prisoner's life for information on the mysteries of agriculture. His British/Welsh counterpart, Lleu, is the yellow-haired son of the Goddess Arianrhod, whom we met at Midsummer. Like Lugh, Lleu is both Sun God and God of Grain.

Lughnasadh (pronounced *loo-na-sa)* marks the beginning of the grain harvest, the first harvest on the Wheel of the Year. The importance of grain to life is evident in virtually every deity structure in every religion on Earth. The entire preparation of grain from seed to harvest parallels the life-in-death and death-in-life aspects of the Great Goddess, Mother Earth.

Celtic mythology is filled with stories that tell of the symbolic significance of grain. In one such myth, a young boy accidentally drinks hazelnuts from the magical cauldron of the Welsh Goddess Cerridwen. He shapeshifts into a hare. She shapeshifts into a greyhound and chases him. He

shapeshifts into a grain of wheat, but then Cerridwen, in turn, shapeshifts into a black hen. She eats the wheat and gives birth to a boy, who becomes the great bard and seer-poet, Taliesin. Cerridwen, then, is Goddess of Death and Regeneration, Grain, and Poetic Inspiration.

The Triple Goddess Macha in her warrior aspect often presides over the Lughnasadh festival. She is forced to race against the King of Ulster's horses while she is pregnant. She gives birth to twins. As she delivers, she curses that the men of Ulster shall experience the pain of child labor for five days and four nights. Through victory in battle, Macha becomes Queen of Ulster for seven years. Her right to the throne is challenged, but she retains her sovereignty by persuading her challengers with her charms. The men build her a fortress, called Emain Macha, which she marks out with a magical brooch of Celtic knotwork. Macha not only presides over battle in war, but also in love. She is concerned with any kind of conflict and its resolution. Macha shapeshifts into a crow—a common appearance on both a battlefield and in the cornfields of Summer.

EARTH MAGIC

By Lughnasadh, the Sun God has already begun his downward journey, facing now toward the dark frosts of Winter. The Goddess, however, never wanes. She simply changes appearance. At Lughnasadh, She wears a face of exquisite abundance. During this season of high Summer the bounty of our planet is in full swing. We reap the benefits of fresh fruits, vegetables, and herbs. This is a time when most of us experience exceptionally good health and robust living.

Lughnasadh marks the last heyday of the Sun God. Beneath the Barley Moon and Summer stars we, too, enjoy the expiring passions of the season. Marriages are often entered into at Lughnasadh as well as at Midsummer, and as Robert Burns tells us, it is a "happy night" that he spends among the cornfields with his lover. Lughnasadh is a time when the symbolic aspects of the life-sustaining elements of grain spill over into every part of life.

Preparations

At Lughnasadh, the altar, adorned with a white or gold cloth, is carried outside. To honor and acknowledge the bounty of the Earth, we bring corn, fruits and vegetables, baskets of bread, and bunches of Summer flowers to our outdoor magic space. We light gold and yellow candles to represent the Sun, and add one candle each to represent the colors of the rainbow. A mixture of herbs ruled by the Sun are placed within easy reach on the altar.

For the following ritual you will need apples; bread; wheat; fruits and vegetables in baskets; a cauldron with water and hazelnuts floating in it; Sabbat cakes; a chalice; salt; water; Cerridwen Oil; Taliesin Oil; Lugh Oil (see p. 215); gold, yellow, white, and black candles; incense; a Lughnasadh Philtre (see p. 214), a silver branch wand (see p. 17); a blade; a spear. (If you don't have a blade or spear, you can choose a similar object, like a brass letter opener, for example. Charge it in a magic circle and call it a blade or a spear.) You will need any or all of the following sacred woods: holly, oak, hawthorn, ash, willow, alder, rowan, birch, grape vine, ivy, water reed, blackthorn, elder, fir, furze, heather, aspen, and yew.

What to Wear

Although many who attend the Lughnasadh celebration come dressed in white or yellow cotton shorts and sleeveless tops, the High Priestess and High Priest usually wear their traditional black or white robes. The High Priestess wears a flower crown with long, three- to four-foot ribbons in the colors of the rainbow. Some of us paint our faces with sunflowers, adorn our hair with flowers and ribbons, and bring with us magical tools to represent Lugh and other Gods and Goddesses.

The Ritual

High Priestess: *To all who hear me, not even for the sake of your beginnings, your mother and father; not even for your love would I harm thee. But for the sake of Dana, I bring life. I give love. I seek sovereignty of Tara. I enter Tara. The green land spreads before my eyes and the mist rises from the water. The Lady of the Lake gives magic. The sword of enchantment will bring only honor to the knight who protects this land. Here is the power of the* sidhe. *Here in this sword is the power of Dana, great and powerful Dana, who brings dreams to life. I honor you. I am enchanted by your power and the Otherworld.*

The sword is plunged into the cauldron of water by the High Priestess and presented to the High Priest.

High Priestess: *Here is the magic of the* sidhe, *who gives life to this Earth. The apple is red with fire; the corn is golden with life; the oak is green with light. All cherish the bright and glorious Sun. O! great standing stones, which harbor the power of life, sing to us of miracles bright, as bright as the Sun.*

High Priest holds up the silver branch wand and

says: *We are the people of the silver branch. The children of Avalon and the Tuatha de Danaan. Ogma, Dana, the Dagda all come to this holy Tara.*

The High Priest picks up the peyton and faces East: *I call the Dagda, bring your power and might. Come to this Tara. We welcome you.* He faces South and says: *I call Ogma, come bring your might and power, we welcome you.* He faces West and says: *I call Mananaan mac Lir, come bring your power and might to this Tara, we welcome you.* He faces North and says: *I call Gwydion, come bring your power and might to this Tara, we welcome you.*

The High Priestess charges the candles and anoints them with Lugh Oil. She says: *Lugh, Great God of the Golden Spear, bringer of the harvest, you are many skilled. Bring your light to share with us, cast your golden light upon the sacred Tara.*

The High Priest sprinkles incense on the coals and says: *Lugh, your appearance is beauteous to behold. Your tartan is bright silk, your golden helmet has crystals of the four realms. You teach us amulets of protection and power. Show to us your golden spear of power.*

The High Priestess, as she lifts her blade to the sky in both hands, says: *I am sovereign here in the name of Cerridwen. I offer you a throne of power in this Tara. Welcome.*

The High Priest picks up the blade and the High Priestess picks up the chalice, holding it up for all to see. She says: *The magical music of Taliesin has heralded the coming of Lugh. I, Sovereign Queen, welcome Lugh to this chalice.*

The High Priest lifts the blade and says: *Lugh, strike this blade with your golden spear that you may enter this sovereign place, Tara. I draw the golden light of Lugh into this chalice.*

The High Priest places the blade in the chalice. The priestess drinks the holy water and hands it to the priest, then pours the rest into the cauldron with hazelnuts and water. The High Priest stirs it with his finger, then places his fingers to his lips three times and tastes the water, and with this the High Priestess turns to him and says: *I welcome the chase of balance, flee from this realm, but you shall never be from my reach.*

The High Priest walks away from her around the circle.

High Priestess: *Cerridwen, Greyhound, chase the Hare, with golden light this truth will bear the balance of Goddess might eclipse of dark and fair, the never-ending race, the circle end to end. Sun, Moon, face-to-face, shapeshift, blend and bend, the Faery faith doth trace.*

The High Priest says as he walks: *Taliesin, sing to me of cauldrons deep and tales that end in honor.*

High Priestess: *I am in place of the Goddess of Transformation and I call all powers of good to this Earth. I thank the powers of the cauldron and the spear for the bounty we see.*

She picks up her wand and touches the basket and says: *I speak as priestess to charge these herbs, fruits, and grains, blessed are they, blessed are the grounds from which they grow. We ask that all people of the Earth partake of this bounty. Grant us the power to help seed, grow, and feed the Earth and its animals.*

All: *Blessed is Lugh, blessed is Cerridwen, blessed is Taliesin.*

The High Priest and High Priestess together bless the cakes and pass to all in the circle. They say together: *These cakes are the power and spirit of the ancient ones.*

After the cakes are finished, oils are passed around

the circle, and all anoint themselves with oils on their foreheads, wrists, and back of the neck.

The High Priestess raises the spear above her head, and everyone comes to attention. Together the High Priestess and High Priest say: *We raise the cone of power.*

All lift their hands to the sky and kneel on the ground or lie on the ground to touch or kiss the Tara, sacred Earth.

The High Priest then picks up the peyton and faces North and says: *Powerful Gwydion, I bid thee farewell. Come again.* He faces West: *Powerful Mananaan mac Lir, I bid thee farewell. Come again.* He faces South and says: *Powerful Ogma, I bid thee farewell. Come again.* He faces East and says: *Powerful Dagda, I bid thee farewell. Come again.*

The High Priestess releases the four elements and then releases the circle. Those chosen by the priest and priestess may sip the sacred cauldron's water. They hand out sticks and each dips into the cauldron. The rest of the water is kept in a sacred space. The rest of the cakes are left as gifts in the woods or shared with all who attend.

Magical Herbs

Lughnasadh marks a turning point in the Earth's life cycle. Although Summer is hot and bountiful, more visible signs of the Sun's waning strength lie just around the corner in Autumn's fallen leaves. During this time of year, Witches use herbs to bring good fortune and abundance in their cooking, healing, potions, and spellwork. All grains, seeds, herbs, and flowers gathered now can be dried for later use during Winter or for decorating the altars of future Sabbats.

Like herbs, grains are considered sacred and should be harvested with a magically charged "golden" sickle.

In many regions in the northern hemisphere, Lughnasadh is berry-picking time. In the British Isles, bilberries are particularly plentiful. Gathering bilberries at Lughnasadh is an ancient ritual that has bearing upon the Summertime harvest as a whole. If the bilberries are bountiful, the crops will be plentiful. Just about every herb, flower, and grain reaches its peak of color, flavor, and magical potency in Summer. Garlic is a particularly versatile herb that is used for protection against negative energy and to cleanse and purify the body. Marigold helps us to communicate with the Faeries and increases psychic ability. Moss is for financial gain, and at Lughnasadh vervain is used for wealth as well as protection. During this season of marriages, yarrow is a common ingredient in wedding-gift philtres and oils for love and union. Hops, used in flavoring beer and ale, favorite Lughnasadh beverages, are also good for sleeping and healing. Witches make healing compresses and teas from comfrey to enhance the healing of broken bones, scrapes, and bruises.

Following is a list of herbs to use in your magic during the Lughnasadh season:

goldenrod
nasturtium
clover blossom
yarrow
heliotrope
boneset
vervain
Queen Anne's lace
myrtle
rose
peony
sunflower
poppy
milkweed
Irish moss
mushroom
wheat
corn
rye
oat

barley
rice
garlic
onion
basil
mint
aloe
acacia
meadowsweet
apple leaf
raspberry leaf
strawberry leaf
bilberry leaf
blueberry leaf
mugwort
hops
holly
comfrey
marigold
grape vine
ivy
hazelnut
blackthorn
elder
bee pollen

DRYING AND PRESERVING HERBS, SEEDS, AND FLOWERS

To dry herbs: Hang the herbs upside down, loosely gathered in bunches, or spread them out on a fine wire mesh. I usually hang my herbs to dry and cover them gently with cheesecloth to keep the dust off. Herbs should be dried in a dark, ventilated room or cupboard in a temperature range from 70° to 90° F. Most herbs dry within a week, but should be checked periodically before then. The herbs are dry when they are dry to the touch but don't crumble and break. When they are ready, remove the leaves and place immediately in mason jars with sealed lids. Date and label the jars, because herbs look so much alike when they are dried, it is hard to tell one from the other. Then store them in a dark room or cabinet.

To dry seeds: To collect seeds from plants, hang plants upside down over a piece of paper or turn plants upside down inside a brown paper bag until dried seeds drop.

To dry flowers: To dry flowers whole, hang them upside down or suspend them right-side up in wire mesh. You can also place them on a cookie sheet, sprinkle them with salt, and put them in a dry room covered in cheesecloth. Drying could take two days or more, but should be checked periodically. To dry leaves and petals, spread flowers out on a wire mesh, shaking them once in a while to encourage even drying.

Marjoram, basil, mint, parsley, chervil, chives, fennel seed, dill, and lovage among others can be frozen. Gather the herbs in the morning while the dew still clings to their leaves. Give them a good shake and place in freezer bags.

Remember, always consult an herbal sourcebook to determine which herbs are edible and which are not. Some herbs are poisonous and should never be ingested.

Philtres, Incense, and Oils

Summer is the time of many great thunder and lightning storms. Witches often collect the rainwater from storms to use in their magic. This water is charged with the energy of light and sound and can generate strong magical impulses in any philtre, incense, or oil. For protection against damage from a storm, however, use the petals, stems, or leaves from peonies in a philtre you can hang on your roof or from the eaves of your home. At Lughnasadh, we make enough of a philtre to share with everyone at the celebration. The aspects of the Sun are contained in all philtre recipes until the next Lughnasadh, when we create new mixtures. Here are a few suggestions of blends you can use in ritual or with talismans and amulets for Summertime enchantments:

LUGHNASADH INCENSE

dried rose petals
barley
yarrow
Irish moss
wheat
basil
apple leaf
3 drops Cerridwen Oil (see p. 215)
1 drop Lugh Oil (see p. 215)

Mix all ingredients and keep in a magical bag or bowl. To charge, put it in a sacred space or bring to the Lughnasadh ritual for the energy of the Sun, growth, healing, wealth, and protection of the Earth.

LUGHNASADH PHILTRE

yarrow
rose
poppy seeds
mushrooms
barley
basil
raspberry leaf
strawberry leaf
mugwort
heliotrope
comfrey
3 drops Macha Oil, below
3 drops Cerridwen Oil (see p. 215)
3 drops Lugh Oil (see p. 215)

Uses the oils to bind the philtre. Blend all ingredients and keep with you in a magic bag. Tie onto a Lughnasadh Witch's cord, and use in your rituals and spells.

CERRIDWEN OIL

1 dram hazelnut oil
1 dram fir oil
1 dram elder oil

See instructions under Macha Oil, below.

TALIESIN OIL

2 drams hazelnut oil
1 pebble from the base of a standing stone
pinch bee pollen
1 tiny feather
1 dram blackthorn oil

See instructions under Macha Oil, below.

LUGH OIL

1 piece gold, such as gold chain or piece of jewelry or shaved gold, which you can get from a jeweler
1 dram heliotrope oil
1 dram sunflower oil
1 citrine stone

See instructions under Macha Oil, below.

MACHA OIL

1 dram grapeseed oil
1 small piece obsidian
1 dram corn oil
1 piece crow feather

All oils should be warmed on very low heat in an enamel pan. Remove from heat when warmed, and let cool. Place in magic bottles and jars in the colors of the rainbow.

Magical Stones

Our imaginations can be easily taken in by the magical charms of stones. They are simple enough in themselves, yet we watch and touch and remember, sometimes brooding upon their eternal composition. Witches believe that stones, despite their seeming lack of animation, are objects of wisdom and great positive energy and, like water, are one of the purest of all of Nature's forms. For untold centuries we have paid attention to the effect of light on form. The geometric forms of crystals reveal fresh new perspectives that aid us in preparing for the future.

At Lughnasadh, as at all Sabbats, we affirm the time-honored importance of stones as our friends. In addition to prosperity and growth, we seek confidence to face what lies ahead and a strengthening of our bond with Nature. The constancy of each individual stone on Earth centers on a mystical kind of compressed raw energy. Stones contain dynamic qualities and to us they exhibit a magical sensibility seemingly at odds with their concreteness. Within the core of each lies imprisoned, like the Young God himself, the concentrated, exquisite spirit of energy and light. Realizing these truths about the magic of stones is particularly helpful during this turning point on the Wheel of the Year, when we straddle Lughnasadh's amazing paradox of abundance and loss.

Following is a list of stones to use in your Lughnasadh magic:

cat's-eye
citrine
adventurine
golden topaz
obsidian
moss agate
rhodochrosite
clear quartz
marble
slate
granite
lodestone

Magical Spells

Around Lughnasadh, Witches cast spells for connectedness, career, health, and financial gain. It is important, however, to realize how the Sun is changing at this point, gradually growing weaker as August approaches September. This is a time to do grounding and Sun meditations. Visualize the Sun's golden light warming your body. You want to feel the glory of the Sun's energy, and then use it for more mundane spellwork. For example, after meditating on the importance of the Sun and thanking the Goddess and God for their gifts of light and heat, you might cast a spell using the Sun's energy to get a new job or perhaps a material gift of some kind. Asking for money or material gain is not forbidden or looked down upon in our spiritual tradition, as long as doing so does not become an obsession or the primary goal of your life. Extreme wealth or extreme poverty is neither healthy nor natural. Witchcraft, as I see it, strives to strike a balance between poverty and wealth. Here are two examples of spells to try at Lughnasadh followed by a Macha meditation and spell:

Lughnasadh Spell for Abundance and Protection

You will need:

1 gold altar cloth
1 white, 1 black, and 1 brown candle
altar facing east
1 wooden staff or wheat chaff
handful of barley and hay
Lugh Oil (see p. 215)
Macha Oil (see p. 215)
Lughnasadh Incense (see p. 214)
1 Celtic brooch or pin dedicated to Macha
3 crow feathers
handful of dried earth from a place you call home
9 inches red ribbon
1 thurible
1 cauldron or bowl

Facing East in front of the altar say: *As the brooch of Macha marks her fortress, I mark this sacred space.* Cast the circle with the staff or chaff of wheat. Invoke the four quarters, elements, or totems. Anoint the candles with Lugh Oil. Light the black and white candles. On the brown candle, carve an initial or rune with the brooch to represent who or what is to be protected. Wrap the base of the candle with the red ribbon and say: *I ask that the warmth of the Sun's rays stay throughout the year to warm our hearts and homes. Grant that we may feel the energy of the Sun in our fields so that they may grow plentiful and feed all the Earth's children.*

Put the incense in the thurible atop the dry soil and light, while saying: *Macha, fly high over this space and protect this my sovereignty, my domain that you have generously granted me. I ask that your brooch mark my space and protect it as your own.*

In the cauldron place the hay and barley and repeat: *As we feast in the good times, Mother, feed us in the hard times. Not just our bodies but our minds. Let us know your bountiful love that warms us like the summer sun.*

Take the crow feathers in your right hand and charge the articles on the altar, moving hands clockwise over the objects, and say: *Macha, who is with us in triplicity as Mother, Maiden, and Crone, stay with us so that we may know all aspects of your love and fruitfulness as well as the strength and protection of the warrior goddess who stands fast against oppression. As she cradles her children to her bosom, I ask that this be correct and for the good of all. So mote it be.*

When the fire fades away, place the incense and soil along with the ribbon and feathers in the cauldron. Put three drops of Macha oil in and mix. Place in a brown magic bag to carry with you or place at the threshold of your entryway. The rest can be saved until needed. Release the quarters and open the circle.

LUGHNASADH BIRD SPELL

Sometimes while walking in Salem Common a shadowy cluster of feathers flutters from above and falls in my magical path. Usually it's a sea gull feather, but sometimes a crow feather finds its way by. There are days when we will walk upon feathers and never notice them. At other times they attract our psychic senses and become omens. *Scrying* originally meant the psychic interpretation of the flight of birds. The word *scry* changed over time to mean divination in general. There is magical meaning in finding feathers. In ancient times, we would wrap gifts with feathers to give secret messages. Brown and white and black mean friendship. A red feather means great fortune, and so on. While using your magical senses, take a stroll and find and collect feathers. Gather magical objects and feathers that you can sew or tie to a magical cord. Here is a cord to attract love and luck on Lughnasadh:

You will need:

2 bluejay feathers
2 crow feathers
1 blue candle
1 blue 3-foot cord
1 white 3-foot cord
1 black 3-foot cord
1 small blue bottle
1 dram Faery Flower Oil (see p. 181)
1 needle and blue thread

Place all items on the altar, anoint the candle with Faery Flower Oil, light it, and say: *Light that glistens on the wings of magical birds, come to my sacred space.*

Put all three cords together and tie a loop at the top. Visualize your future very bright and visualize yourself receiving riches, health, a clean environment, and a love in your life. Shapeshift into a bird. Fly over the Earth where you live. While flying, say: *Wings of spirit, strengthen me and all I see. The wind under my wing blows for good, and fortunate things are for me and the Earth.*

Return to your space and braid the cords, chanting: *Health, wealth, love, and safety.* After you've said it three times, tie a knot. Then sew or glue a feather into the cord where the knot is. Tie a small bottle filled with Faery Flower Oil onto your cord, and continue braiding and placing your feathers. Hold the finished cord in your hands and charge the cord with your intentions once more (once more visualizing yourself with love and health, for example). Then release the circle and hang the cord in your living or work space.

MACHA MEDITATION AND SPELL

Sit in a comfortable position. Count into alpha. Visualize yourself on the back of a crow. Feel its feathers close to your body. You are soaring through the breeze. Feel the wind on your face and billowing through your robes. You float through the clouds and you see below you fields in the bright sunlight. There are people singing as they rake the hay into mounds in the hot sun. You are now so close you can smell the fresh hay and hear the lilt of a harvester's song. Alight in a nearby oak tree. Macha sits to the right of the field and She protects all She surveys. The Sun of Lugh is high in the sky, but the strength of the Sun is waning. There is a sense of peace and security as you are wrapped in Macha's wings. Rest. You are in her arms, the wings of the Mother, and basking in the warmth of the Father's rays.

Cast the following spell, saying out loud:

> *On the wings of the crow, Macha watches the gathering of the fruits and grains. The mowing of the hay excites Her senses and the tribe gathers for the feast. Mother, Macha, Crone of the harvest, join us as we give thanks for this bounty. Partake and bless our abundance. So mote it be.*

HOLIDAY FARE

Lughnasadh is a time of great bounty. Juicy red tomatoes can be eaten right off the vine. Trees and vines are heavy with ripened fruits and vegetables. In each meal we eat, we experience the exquisite contrast between the freshness of fruits, vegetables, and herbs and their dried or canned Winter counterparts. At the Lughnasadh feast, all food should be the freshest available, vegetable leaves deep green and crisp and fruits sweet and juicy. Magic adds a marvelous quality and spiritual dimension to a meal that makes it different and exciting. For example, it enhances your entire meal to know that the nasturtiums in the wild herb salad (given below) give off tiny beams of light at dusk!

The following menu is typical of an American Summertime cookout, but remember there are rarely any set rules in a Witch's culinary repertoire, other than to do your best to eat foods native to your region. Magically prepared food, however, should reflect your own personality and desires for the future. If beef or lamb are too fatty for you or you simply don't like the taste, substitute grilled turkey patties that are low in fat and cholesterol, or chicken or fish. If wild herbs and flowers have too strong a taste for you in a salad, substitute a fresh vegetable salad using cucumbers, tomatoes, and mushrooms. The important part of preparing and enjoying a magically made meal is to thank the Goddesses and Gods for the eternal bounty of the land and then to eat, drink, and make merry! Following are a few suggestions of what to serve:

FEAST OF LUGH

Rose Petal Wine
Corn Bread Sabbat Cakes
Beef or Lamb Patties
Wild Herb Salad with Vinaigrette
Roasted Corn on the Cob
Berries and Cream

ROSE PETAL WINE

4–5 roses, organically grown
1 large carafe of wine

Remove petals from rose stems, gently rinse in a colander, and place in the bottom of empty glass carafe. Please make sure roses have been organically grown without the use of pesticides. Pour wine of your choice over rose petals and serve.

CORN BREAD SABBAT CAKES

¾ cup sifted flour
2½ tsp. baking powder
2 tbs. sugar
¾ tsp. salt
1½ cups cornmeal
1 egg, beaten
3 tbs. melted butter or margarine
1 cup milk

Grease a 9 × 9-inch baking pan and place (without the cornbread batter inside) in preheated oven at 475° F. Sift together flour, baking powder, sugar, salt, and cornmeal. Add egg, melted butter, and milk. Blend by hand. Do not overmix. Place batter in hot pan. Bake at 475° F for 25 minutes or until top is golden brown.

BEEF OR LAMB PATTIES

4 lbs. ground beef or lamb
¼ cup bread crumbs
1 tsp. basil
1 tsp. parsley
1 tsp. lemon juice

1 onion, chopped fine
1 slice white bread, soaked in 1/4 cup milk

Combine all ingredients in a large bowl. Shape into 1/4- to 1/2-inch-thick patties. Broil for about 10 minutes on each side or grill to desired doneness.

WILD HERB SALAD WITH VINAIGRETTE

4 nasturtium flowers and 16 leaves
12 red clover blossoms
4 sprigs basil
4 sprigs rosemary
4 kale leaves
4 purple mustard leaves
12 violet leaves
8 dandelion leaves

Toss all ingredients in a large salad bowl charged with the energy of the Sun.

FOR THE DRESSING:

4 tbs. olive oil
2 tbs. balsamic vinegar
1/2 tsp. minced garlic

ROASTED CORN ON THE COB

Fresh ears of corn
water
butter
salt and pepper

Pull down husks on corn without pulling off. Remove silk threads. Rinse corn with water. Rub with butter, salt, and pepper. Replace husks, twisting them to secure. Place in oven at 400° F for 25 minutes or on grill for the same amount of time.

BERRIES AND CREAM

½ lb. fresh strawberries
½ lb. fresh blueberries
½ lb. fresh raspberries (if available)
½ lb. fresh blackberries
1 pt. whipping cream (heavy cream)
1 tsp. sugar

Toss berries in a large bowl. Whip cream in a small bowl with beaters that have been chilled in refrigerator for 2 hours. Whip until the cream is thick and light and forms stiff peaks.

ANCIENT ACTIVITIES

In ancient times the last chaff of wheat or grain to be cut was kept and crafted into a corn dolly. At Lughnasadh, she is called Corn Mother and is kept in a magical, sacred space. On Imbolc, Lughnasadh's opposite on the Wheel of the Year, she becomes Corn Bride, the Maiden Goddess Brid, and is used in our holiday ritual. Grain necklaces and bracelets can be strung and worn as amulets of fertility and protection. Wreaths are often made during this time of year, for the same purposes, from grain heads and corn husks. To these we often add the blossoms of Summer that from ancient times grew here, their sweet blossoms in their seasons, giving up their perfumes for all to enjoy.

Lughnasadh is a time of robust health and erotic energy. The ancient tribes met during this time of the year to gather news, settle any disputed arguments, arrange marriages, and show off strength and skill. They held sporting events and horse races, picked berries, frolicked in the fields, played board games, and crafted amulets and talismans by braiding strands of onions and garlic. It is also the perfect time to make oils and vinegars from fresh flowers and herbs. These are great gifts to give at Winter Solstice or on Imbolc.

FLOWER AND HERB OILS AND VINEGARS

To make scented flower and herb oils, fill halfway with an oil of your choice—olive oil, safflower oil, or sunflower oil—a mason jar or special magic bottle that can be sealed. Add sea salt to the bottom to keep the fresh sprigs of flowers and herbs from turning rancid. Once the oil is opened, keep it refrigerated. Add any culinary herb or flower you like. Sprigs of rosemary, basil, or thyme work well. Or skewer whole garlic cloves with tiny skewers so the cloves won't break. Fill the remaining jar with oil and seal. Do the same for vinegars. You can use a gourmet vinegar or simply buy plain white vinegar from the grocer. Float the herbs in the vinegar and add galangal root for scent. You can skewer garlic cloves or onions to make garlic and onion vinegar as well. The longer the oil or vinegar sits, the more it becomes infused with the herb or flower. Vinegars work well in corked bottles. To seal a corked bottle using beeswax, turn the bottle over into a pan of melted wax on a low flame. Tie a beautiful Witch's cord around the neck, attach a parchment tag that labels the oil or vinegar, and you have a wonderful Faery garden gift for any occasion.

WITCHES REDUCE, REUSE, AND RECYCLE!

Witches have respected the planet long before the arrival of Greenpeace and GreenTeens and long before the ecology-minded individuals of the so-called New Age movement. Honoring, loving, and nurturing the Earth is not simply a political stance for a Witch. Indeed, it is even more than a religion. Witchcraft is a way of life. The notions of saving and recycling were brought over to America by Witches and are evident in many of the practices of early American farmers. Most Witches keep a year and a half's worth of food and water in their homes, preparing themselves for the cycles of the seasons. One year the Salem water pipes broke and the entire town was without water for seven days. Mine was one of the few households prepared for such an emergency. Here are two recipes you can use to ensure that you have at least the basics on hand in case of an emergency.

GRAIN SAVER

To save grain, add one tablespoon fossil flour to the bottom of an airtight jar. (Fossil flour can be obtained in most health food stores.) This prevents bugs and mites from hatching and keeps grain fresh.

WATER SAVER

To save water, add five drops of chlorine bleach to a one- or two-gallon jug. This keeps water fresh for five months. Date and label the jugs, rotating your stock at the end of the five-month period. Figure one to two gallons of water per person per household per day.

Faery Magic

At Lughnasadh, Witches like to call upon the skilled and gifted members of the Faery faith. Sometimes when the Moon is doing strange and wonderful things and we wonder at the secrets of the stars, it helps to celebrate the constancy of the Faeries. Their lively spirits infuse all of Nature with Otherworldly vitality. This diverse pantheon of Goddesses and Gods is filled with animated figures of youth and entrancing harmonies. They are accomplished and visionary and feed our love of beauty and the magical arts.

In Celtic legend, the Catti People of Ireland were one such tribe. The Catti, or Cat People, were a mystical people who worshipped cats and emulated cats in the way they made up their faces. If a cat died, they wore the catskin as a sacred cloak. They would keep the fur to make headdresses and wear the claws as amulets. The Celts believed the eyes of the cat were an entrance to the Faery world. A cat's brain is always in alpha, so it is very easy to communicate with psychically. So-called cat experts would say that cats are hallucinating when they stare at certain spots in the room. We know they are seeing the spirit world. Cats become familiars the more you pet them. You can go into alpha and work with them and talk to them a lot. I have three cats who allow me to live in my house. They are great company and have undying love. I often use them in my magic. If you would like to communicate with the Faery world, especially with a King or Queen, cats are good communicators. Here is some cat potion you can use to anoint your cat, bringing him or her protection and magical empowerment, followed by a cat spell given in honor of the Catti tribe from Ireland.

CAT POTION

1 dram catnip oil
1 dram heliotrope oil
large pinch catnip leaves
1 dram olive oil
shedding fur from a live magic cat (just a few strands)

Blend all ingredients and keep in a magic bottle.

CAT SPELL

Putting a cat in the Magic Circle is not always a good idea, because during a ritual they often decide to get up and leave to have a snack. It is better to use fur or whiskers to represent the cat in the circle. Never cut a cat's whiskers! They use their whiskers to judge the width of their bodies. Gather them up when they fall out. For the following spell you will need:

cat potion, above
1 statue or picture of a cat
1 white, 1 black, 1 green, and 1 yellow candle
1 small bowl
1 thurible and charcoal
Faery Flower Oil (see p. 181)
1 magic mirror
1 bowl cat food or sliced chicken or turkey for special treat
1 wand
1 black magic bag
3-foot black cord
parchment
1 black pen

Light the candles and anoint with cat potion, and say: *I call upon the clan of the Cat People to come to this sacred space and bring their power and love to cast a Faery spell.*

Put Faery Flower Oil on coal and say: *Faery magic play and pat upon the magic of this cat.*

Pick up the picture or cat statue and pass it through the smoke of the incense. Place "cat" in front of the magic mirror as if the cat were looking into it. On your parchment write:

"Catti, Catti, show to me what my future is to be. Catti, Catti, to me send a future I may shape and bend. Catti, Catti, protect the animals and the human race. I ask that this will be approved in the eyes of the *sidhe,* by my will. So mote it be."

Place some cat fur, Faery Flower Oil, whiskers, and three drops of cat potion on the spell. Roll it up and put it in the black magic bag. Then tie the bag to the black cord so you may wear it for three days and nights. While you wear the black bag, expect your cat to act a little strange. She will see the Faeries around you. When you have a chance, pet her and look into her eyes to see the Otherworld. If you do not have a cat, use the statue or picture and keep it in front of your magic mirror every time you need an answer or protection. After the three days and nights, hang the cord in your living space.

If you want, you can make a cat collar, taking black fabric and forming a tiny tube to fit around his neck. Place tiny crystals or some herbs inside. Or buy a collar and tie on a pentacle, but charge it in a Magic Circle first.

MABON
Autumn Equinox
(around September 22nd)

★

As humans, I believe we are tied by a bond of empathy with the destiny of our planet, Earth. Whether we consciously choose to acknowledge the bond from the point of view of our daily lives matters little to our spiritual, emotional, and biological selves, who must act in accordance with an inner necessity. These essential impulses are commanded, of course, by the eternal ebb and flow of Life, the cosmic laws and harmonies that return us to Earth's beginnings. During the September Equinox, when the Sun passes our planet's equator, making night and day of almost equal length all over the world, I feel in a passionate sense the extraordinary relationship between humankind and these primordial movements, patterns, and tides. The influence of so gentle a turn in the Earth's axis, a poetic motion established long before the existence of time, is profound.

THE STORY OF MABON

At this point on the Wheel of the Year, I choose to celebrate the universal story of Mabon, which has been passed down to us from the ancient proto-Celtic oral tradition. Mabon ap Modron, meaning "son," or "son of the mother," is the Young Son, Divine Youth, or, as I prefer to call him,

Son of Light. Just as the September Equinox marks a significant time of change, so, too, does the birth of Mabon. Modron is his mother, the Great Goddess, Guardian of the Otherworld, Protector, and Healer. She is Earth itself.

From the moment of the September Equinox, the Sun's strength diminishes, until the moment of Winter Solstice in December, when the Sun grows stronger and the days once again become longer than the nights. Mabon also disappears, taken at birth when only three nights old. His mother is in sweet lament. And though his whereabouts are veiled in mystery, Mabon is eventually freed with the help of the wisdom and memory of the most ancient of living animals—the Blackbird, the Stag, the Owl, the Eagle, and the Salmon. His seeker asks the ritual question of each totem animal: "Tell me if thou knowest aught of Mabon, the son of Modron, who was taken when three nights old from between his mother and the wall?"

All along, however, Mabon has been dwelling, a happy captive, in Modron's magical Otherworld—Modron's womb. It is a nurturing and enchanted place, but also one filled with challenges. Only in so powerful a place of renewable strength can Mabon be reborn as his mother's champion, the source of joy and Son of Light. Mabon's light has been drawn into the Earth, gathering strength and wisdom enough to become a new seed.

To understand the themes of Mabon's story is to accept the reality and significance of an archetypal world. The archetypes of Mabon and Modron are first forms or first models that allow us to consider information not strictly measurable by machines or the physical senses. They transcend the boundaries of convention and can travel, as the entire pantheon of Goddesses and Gods travels, between the worlds. Witches, like the Celts, who also practiced Witchcraft, have a deeply held sense of coexistent, multiple time dimensions. There are many cycles of time, and many of the cycles overlap. We believe in our history, but we also believe in the presence of truth outside of time.

The story of Mabon and Modron, because it is archetypal, echoes through all ages and is for all beings of all religions in all worlds. There are many Mabons and many Modrons. The Greek god Apollo shares many of Mabon's characteristics. Mabon's Gaulish title is Maponus. Mabon was celebrated along Hadrian's Wall, and there is new evidence that he was honored long before the arrival of the Vikings in North America! (See below.) Although much was changed, aspects of Mabon and Modron are found in the later Jewish and Christian religions.

Each of our cultural identities comes from how we interpret and position ourselves in these narratives of the past. During the September Equinox, this dramatic moment of cosmic balance as well as change, I honor Mabon and the Great Goddess, his mother, Modron, in ritual. The ritual that follows is from the Cabot tradition and a part of the liturgy reclaimed by the Temple of Nine Wells in Salem, Massachusetts. This is offered as an example. You can and are encouraged to make up one of your own.

THE CELTS WERE IN AMERICA!

Hard evidence has been found that the Celtic Gods and Goddesses were worshiped right here in America long before the arrival of the Vikings and Christopher Columbus. Until now, so much of our history was lost to or confused with Native American legend and lore. In his remarkable, precedent-setting book *America B.C.: Ancient Settlers in the New World,* Harvard professor Barry Fell relates the stunning archaeological discoveries of Celtic altars, standing stones carved in ogam (the Celtic alphabet), libation bowls, and other ritual artifacts that date from 800–600 B.C.! Dolmens were discovered in Massachusetts, and a Beltane Stone dating from the time of Julius Caesar was found in Mystery Hill, New Hampshire. A stone monument built to align with Winter Solstice was uncovered in Danbury, Connecticut. Nearby, other structures were found inscribed in ogam honoring the Celtic Sun God, Bel. Altars carved in ogam that celebrate Mabon, the Young God, were discovered in South Woodstock, Vermont; and a wooden mask of the Horned God, Cernunnos, among many other artifacts, was unearthed in Oklahoma—the place of my birth—at Spiro Mound. The Celts in America left a trail of inscriptions and burial mounds as they journeyed up the Mississippi, Arkansas, and Cimarron rivers! Thanks to Barry Fell's exhaustive and epic research into America's prehistory, for the first time we now have scientific proof of something so many American Witches only half believed or dreamed about—that, yes, the Celts most definitely were here! This is why I feel the power of Merlin in the old woods of Lenox, Massachusetts, and the Faery power in my garden. And this may be why most people find the shamanic practices of Native Americans so similar to Witchcraft traditions.

EARTH MAGIC

Long ago, in many parts of the world, the Witch holiday of Mabon was usurped into Harvest Home celebrations. Hardworking farmhands brought in the harvest and shared the feast. The spiritual aspects were—and are still today—either suppressed, forgotten, or lost. This is unfortunate for us and our planet. Rituals, in general, help to reconnect us with a heightened sense of spirituality. By participating we become more fluent in communing with experiences that often defy understanding in the physical world. In a ritual we can balance reality or our position in everyday society with Nature. We might discover the need for a change in our lives, or we might convey a passionate commitment to protect our environment. Rituals are insightful, empathetic, and enjoyable.

The Mabon ritual puts us in touch with the transformational elements of life here on Earth. This is a bittersweet stop on the ever-turning Wheel of the Year. The September Equinox is a beautiful, natural phenomenon worthy of our recognition and honor. It is sad, though, to realize that throughout history we've been kept from taking part in and enjoying so simple a celebration. And so, on this particular holiday, we cry and we laugh. The Son of Light is changing, and the Goddess Mother laments. We, as priestesses, wear little tears on our faces. Some of us literally cry, mourning the gradual disappearance of the Sun, but then we immediately rejoice and thank the Mother for giving birth to the Son, for holding him in Her womb, and for nurturing him.

The Mabon ritual carries the wisdom of the ages and hopefully divine inspiration, which will give sacred life and meaning to the many challenges and changes we face, and to the light and shadows around us.

Preparations

While the basic setup of the altar remains the same, the colors and a few magical tools, in true Mabon fashion, change. During Mabon, you want to decorate the altar in autumn colors such as gold, orange-red, russet, copper, and bronze. Dried ferns, marigold, milkweed, wheat, ash leaf, laurel leaf, cat-o'-nine-tails, and thistle may also be used around Mabon-tide to decorate the altar. You might have a bowl of oak leaves or acorns, which help to empower your magic, on the altar. Baskets of gourds, grains, pumpkins, and fruit should be nearby.

In addition to the black and white candles on the left and right side respectively, we often add a gold or yellow candle to the left and a brown or red-orange candle to the right. Two chalices of spring water and a dish of salt between them represent the tears of the Goddess. You will also need a ritual blade, a large staff, a chaff of wheat, and fruit either on the altar or in a basket. The altar on Mabon faces West, where the Sun sinks. On Mabon the altar cloth is usually gold, but it may be any color appropriate for this particular time of year. You will also need a peyton, a golden or bronze sickle, Mabon Oil and Incense for Prosperity (see pp. 244–46), charcoal, a thurible, and altar matches. Remember to use wooden matches with no advertising of any kind on the box; there should not be any kind of writing other than spellwriting in the circle.

What to Wear

The High Priestess wears a crown decorated in oak leaves, grain, and acorns with flowing orange, bronze, and gold ribbons. An apple, representing the Goddess, sits in the crown's center. We paint blue tears on our faces to represent Modron's tears for Her son. As a priestess I always wear ritual black robes to draw in light. On Mabon, I add to my dress the colors of the Sun and Earth, sometimes by wearing a stole of orange, wine, yellow, and brown trimmed in gold for the Sun. If you are good at sewing or embroidering, you might stitch or appliqué the Sun and Earth symbols on your clothing. The symbol for Earth is a brown diamond shape. The Sun is represented by a gold circle with a dot in the middle. You might embroider the runes for Mother, Earth, Sun, protection, life, and rebirth. You might also use liquid embroidery, which can be purchased at a crafts shop, to paint on symbols and runes. The High Priest wears oak leaves, wheat, herbs, and colored ribbons on his crown or headpiece.

The Ritual

Mabon and Modron play out one of the major dramas on the Wheel of the Year. Their holiday is an emotional time of joy and sorrow. As Modron transforms the life of Her son, Mabon, we feel and endure the polarity of human emotions. This event is purposeful. Death and rebirth are comforting in view of the Great Mother's ability to continue life beyond death. Nothing in the world is more tragic than a mother losing the life of a child. And nothing is sweeter than the growth of a child in the womb.

Autumn in New England is ablaze with orange, pink, yellow, and wine-red leaves against the dark green of balsam and pine trees. The sky is always bright blue, and gentle, crisp breezes often stir and fly the fallen leaves. Orange pumpkins and gourds can be seen on hillsides as farmers harvest and place them to sell on roadside stands and carts, along with ripe red apples and dried corn. You can almost naturally feel the balance as the Sun crosses the equator. The rhythm of change is holy and it balances us physically and spiritually. We can truly know and feel we are in time with the flow of life as we unite with the spirit of all.

Now we set ourselves to do magic, and to deepen our commitment to life and our faith. We, too, can change like the seasons and better our world and all in it. We achieve this through ritual and celebration. The ritual places each of us as being at one with the Goddess and God. We know more profoundly of their existence and power by doing their work here on Earth. In ritual we receive glimpses and flickers of the power of the Goddess and God, which we embody. In these ecstatic moments of magic, we are the universe.

Before setting an altar or stepping into a Magic Circle, you should reflect upon a balancing meditation of some kind. You will need to meditate on the meaning of your life and magic at this turn on the Wheel. Take a long walk in your autumn environment. Kick up the leaves as you did when you were a child. Sit on a log and watch the clouds make shapes for you to scry or divine. Think of the lost Summer Sun and the chilling Winter of ice and snow that is coming. Ask yourself these questions: Am I ready to face change? Am I ready to create warmth in a time of winter on this Earth and in my life? Can I bring light back to a dark situation if one occurs? Why do the seasons change? Does the change take place within me as well as without? Have I the power to change? Am I wise to sense change, loss, and gain? What is my harvest? What is there to be thankful for in my family, community, or world at large?

Two hours before the time of the equinox, take a warm bath. Use herbal oils if you wish, dress in your ritual clothing and jewelry, and prepare to set the altar in Mabon fashion.

The High Priestess casts the circle three times clockwise and says the following:

I cast this circle and create a sacred space, a gateway to the Otherworld. This circle shall protect us from all negative and positive energies and forces that may come to do harm. The first ring I cast is black, the second is white, and the third is gold. So mote it be.

As she lifts her arms upward to the universe, the High Priestess says:

I am sovereign here in this land. My castle is the home of magic and mist, of woods and lands, of great beauty. In this land the Goddess reigns and Her son is paramount. The Faeries roam this land and mournful music fills the air this day, at this hour. Modron, O! great Queen and Earth Mother, we call you here to share your sorrow.

High Priest: *O! shadowed God, great son of Modron, we plead your return from the mysterious world that keeps you. The power of your brilliance is the joy of your mother. Modron is Earth and the Mother we all attend. Her bittersweet lament nurtures your return to be born again and again.*

The priest uses his ritual blade to lift a bit of salt from the dish into one of the chalices of spring water and says:

The salt of your tears is upon our face.

The priest mixes the salt in the water, lifts the chalice, dips his finger into the chalice, touching it to the priestess's face, then to his own face. Then the priestesses and chanters often sob, feeling the loss of the child, and they sometimes even cry. The priestess charges, anoints, and lights the candles and incense and sprinkles some of the incense onto the hot charcoal. As she lights the candles, she says:

I light these candles to draw back to Earth the light of the Sun.

The priestess then takes a small packet of wheat

stalks in her left hand and in her right hand a golden sickle. She raises them to the sky and speaks:

The tip of this sickle is the gleaming light of Mabon.

She then strikes the wheat with the sickle and places them on the altar.

High Priest: *We thank the God and Goddess for the bounty we enjoy, which sustains life on Earth.*

In front of the altar is a basket of bread, wheat, and fruits of all kinds. The priest and priestess walk to the basket, picking up pieces of fruit, lifting them up to the sky to say together:

We give thanks to our ancient ones. We give thanks to our God and Goddess who shower us with great blessings at this time of the great harvest.

They each put down the fruit and walk to the altar. The priestess picks up the chalice of spring water. The priest picks up the ritual blade, raising the blade toward the Sun.

High Priestess: *We rejoice at your return, Mabon. Welcome to the Earth as infant and seed. Welcome.*

All in the circle repeat: *Welcome.*

High Priest: *With this blade I draw down into this sacred chalice and water the energy of the Sun. As the night is to day, the male to female, I charge this chalice with the energy of the God and Goddess. Unite. So mote it be.*

The priest places the blade in the water. Both close their eyes to visualize the light of the Sun entering the water of the chalice. They open their eyes. The priest places the blade on the altar and the priestess lifts the cup to be shown around the circle. She sips from the water and hands the cup to the priest, who takes a sip of the holy water.

High Priestess: *We are all blessed and are grateful. We shall rejoice and feast on the awakenings of this harvest.*

High Priest and High Priestess together: *We now raise the cone of power.*

All participating follow the priest and priestess as they lift their hands from their sides to the sky, then bend down and place both hands on the Earth.

All: *Blessed is the Earth.*

Everyone rises. The priest or priestess picks up the peyton, holds it first to the West, then to the East, North, and South. He places it on the altar. The priestess picks up the wand. She walks widdershins, or counterclockwise, holding the wand extended, and says:

This circle is released into the cosmos to do our bidding. This circle is undone but not broken. So mote it be.

All participants laugh, hug, and rejoice. The Wheel has been turned once more for a better life.

Magical Herbs

The herbs of Mabon offer us the perfect chance to share in the joys of this enchanted season and in the bounty of Mother Earth. As the cooler days and nights of autumn arrive, the vivid greens and bright blooms of herbs, plants, and flowers begin to fade, changing into darker shades of brown, copper, golden yellow, and bronze. An herb should be used when its magical strength is at its peak. If its roots are to be used, cut it just before the plant is about to die. If its blooms or leaves are to be used, cut it just before it is about to bud. During Mabon the Sun's energy is being drawn back into the earth, into the roots of the herb, where most of its magical power is now stored.

When Witches gather herbs, we cut them with a golden (or bronze) sickle that we have charged in a Magic Circle. As we have said, the freshly cut herb should never touch the ground. If it does, its magical energy is returned to the Mother. During the autumn season, we save acorns and all the herbs, grains, and seeds we can find, either for drying and storing or for cultivating indoors for reseeding in the Spring. Around this time, generally any herb that is dying and is ruled by the Sun is appropriate to use in philtres, potions, or brews.

Following is a list of some of the more common herbs and plants used during Mabon:

rue
yarrow
rosemary
marigold
sage
walnut leaves and husks
mistletoe
saffron
chamomile
almond leaves
passionflower
frankincense
rose hips
bittersweet
sunflower
wheat
oak leaves
dried apple or apple seeds

We often dry herbs at Mabon as well as at Lughnasadh (see p. 212). Witches are always prepared for the cycles of the seasons. The custom of preserving, drying, pickling—not only herbs but grains, fruits, and vegetables—is a Witch tradition. Mabon is the time to check your herb closets, cellars, and larders. How well you've prepared will determine how well you will live during the Winter. When the harvest is good, we reap the bounty, share our food, and save all that we can for the colder months ahead or for another time, perhaps next Summer, when the harvest is not so plentiful.

Philtres, Incense, and Oils

Mixing marigold, passionflower, and fern, and using frankincense or myrrh as a resin will make a beautiful incense to burn during Mabon. An herbal blend of dried yarrow and rosemary can be set out as a magical blend in order to bring the warmth of the Sun inside. Make a Mabon Philtre out of dried yarrow and bittersweet to attract love and protection. Add a tiny crystal or a piece of gold jewelry, perhaps a single gold earring you've lost the mate to, and you'll be welcoming the sunlight, honoring Mabon, and taking part in the beauty of the September Equinox.

Any proportion of Mabon herbs can be used in making philtres, oils, or incense. Experiment. Make up your own amounts and proportions according to how you feel or what you're trying to achieve. If you are concerned about the aromatherapy of an oil or incense, keep trying different formulas until you arrive at a scent that is pleasant to you. Following are some suggestions for blends that work well around Mabon:

MABON OIL

You may purchase Mabon Oil from a High Priestess or Witch supply shop (see Sources). To make your own, combine equal parts of the following (but if you do not want to use both, you may use either one or the other):

hazelnut oil *almond oil*

ADD:

pinch marigold leaves
walnut shells, usually crushed or in pieces
pinch oak leaves
1 acorn
1 stone ruled by the Sun (such as yellow topaz, citrine, cat's-eye, amber)

Mix all ingredients in an enamel pan. Slowly warm the oil. Turn it off and let it cool. Place it into a bottle, bowl, or saucer that will only be used to charge oils in your Magic Circle. To charge the oil itself, bring it into a Magic Circle at Mabon time or during your Mabon ritual. Some Witches raise their ritual blade or small wand and ask the Goddess and God to strike the blade or wand with light and power to charge this magical oil. When you have completed this, release your circle.

MABON PHILTRE OR INCENSE FOR PROSPERITY AND PROTECTION

In a bowl only to be used to mix this Mabon philtre, blend 3 tablespoons each:

marigold
dried oak leaves
fern
passionflower
frankincense
myrrh
dried apple
yarrow
rosemary
bittersweet
wheat

ADD:

1 dram Mabon Oil (see p. 244)
1 tsp. of shiny gold glitter, or a piece of real gold jewelry

Mix well. Place the bowl in your magic space or Magic Circle so it will be charged. Place on a table or cabinet in your home or office, use in your prosperity spell (see Magical Spells, p. 98), or burn it as a Mabon incense.

Magical Stones

Stones, especially crystals, are amazing conductors of magical energies. For centuries, spirit healers have recognized the abilities of stone, whether gemstone, crystal, or igneous rock, to protect, heal, communicate, and express love and prosperity. During Mabon, stones ruled by the Sun will help bring the Sun's energy to you. Mabon stones include the following:

clear quartz
amber
peridot
diamond
gold (the metal)
citrine
yellow topaz
cat's-eye
adventurine

These can be worn as jewelry or carried in a philtre. Because colder months lie ahead, Mabon is usually a good time to place crystals at the four corners of your home for protection. Witches also use stones to create sacred circles in wooded areas or in their backyards. From the enchanted arrangements found in the Celtic countryside of the "Mighty Island," Great Britain, to the medicine wheels of

Native Americans found in North America, circles of stones signify places of powerful concentrations of energy. Indeed, Earth itself can be seen as one enormous energy-infused rock upon which we walk and dance and sing and breathe in unison, the rhythm of the whole, once again, becoming the rhythm of each.

Mabon Spells

Because Mabon is a time for balance, I often cast spells that will bring into balance and harmony the energies either in a room, home, or situation. Mabon is also a time for change. There is an edge or briskness in the air. A sense of exuberance in anticipation of the change is present, but along with that a vulnerability that comes with any new experience. Around Mabon, I often cast spells not only for protection but for wealth and prosperity, to bring a feeling of self-confidence or security. It often helps me to focus my magical intent by meditating on the Goddess or Young God. Sometimes I write down my thoughts and feelings and sometimes I create a short poem, as I have done for other Sabbats, to concentrate my energies and emotions. Here is a poem I wrote about Mabon, the Young God of Light, who also has many associations with Merlin the Magician:

Prince and Wizard,
Witch, Royal Witch,
who grants love, health, internal strength and power,
give your power from the sacred wells to bring life from stone.
The lament from your Mother, Modron, is truly a tribute for lasting love and power.
O! great standing stone, the Merlin,
youthful and loving son, adieu! adieu!

O! Great Mother, speak your farewell, anew! anew!
As the wheel spins round is marked by the sound,
Anew! anew! Adieu! adieu!
from the wells come the healing powers of Mabon.

Here is a spell that is good for achieving a sense of place or harmony in your life, followed by an herbal prosperity spell.

POLARITY IMBALANCE SPELL

This visualization uses the four elements: Earth, Air, Fire, and Water. Lie down or sit in a comfortable chair and count yourself into alpha (see Appendix, p. 262). Breathe deeply and visualize your own body. In your mind's eye see your legs from the hips down as rich brown earth. As you see your legs as earth, repeat what you see.

Say: *I am earth. Mother Earth is part of me. I am her earth child.*

See and visualize your stomach and hips from the waist to the hip sockets. Fill this area of your body with water. As you visualize the element of water say the following:

Clear and cool, primordial fluid is part of me and I am part of the lakes, oceans, pools, and streams of life.

See your chest from neck to waist as air. Sometimes you may need to visualize clouds to envision air. Then repeat:

I am air, and air is part of me. I have the flight, breath, and freedom of movement. I breathe the universe.

Next, visualize your head from top to neck as fire. As you visualize the flame or glowing heat of fire, you say:

I am Pi, the fire within. I am the Goddess and the God of Light, and the creative force of all. I am all that has been, all that is, and all that shall be.

Stay in alpha and see your entire body in four powerful sections of Earth, Water, Air, and Fire. When you feel it is correct, allow all the elements to mix and stir throughout your body, mind, and spirit. Stay in alpha for a few minutes before counting up, and enjoy the feeling of being totally balanced.

HERBAL PROSPERITY SPELL

Cast a Magic Circle or get into a magic space. Bring with you the following:

- *Mabon Oil (see p. 244)*
- *1 gold or yellow candle*
- *1 black candle*
- *1 pen to write spells*
- *1 tea bag (make sure you remove the tag) of herbal spiced tea that has cinnamon and cloves in it*
- *1 four-inch square of yellow fabric, preferably cotton or silk, or a magic bag*
- *gold or yellow thread or cord*
- *2 tbs. each:*
  - *rosemary*
  - *marigold*
  - *yarrow*
- *1 clear quartz crystal*
- *1 citrine*
- *1 thurible*
- *Mabon Prosperity Incense (see p. 245)*
- *1 instant-light charcoal*
- *1 four-inch square of parchment paper or paper you use for spells and affirmations*

In a Magic Circle, anoint the candles with Mabon Oil or money oil, which can be purchased from a Witch supply shop. Hold the gold candle and charge it with these words: *I charge this candle to bring prosperity to me. I ask that this harms none and that it is correct for all. So mote it be.* Hold the black candle. Say, *I charge this candle to draw to me all that is safe, correct, and granted by the Gods and Goddesses.*

Place the candles in the holders and say as you light them: *This flame is the light of the God Mabon and the Mother Goddess Modron.*

Light the charcoal. Put a pinch of Prosperity Incense on it. Take the piece of parchment paper and write your spell. For example:

"I ask the Goddess Modron and the God Mabon to grant me this: prosperity in all I do, money, health, and happiness. I ask for heightened psychic, spiritual, and physical balance and power. I ask this to be correct in the eyes of the God and Goddess and for the good of all. So mote it be."

Repeat this spell out loud, speaking to the God and Goddess. See them in your sacred space listening to your words. Thank them out loud for the bounty they have given you in the past. Think of the Wheel of the Year that has come before, and be truly thankful for all you have been granted, even if only your own life. Smudge the spell in the smoke of the incense by passing the paper through the rising smoke. Roll the spell and tie with some yellow thread or cord and set it aside. Place the fabric square or magic bag in front of you with some gold cord or thread to tie it. Pick up your dried herbs and stones one by one. Hold them in your hands. Lift your hands up and show them to the God and Goddess. Visualize the light of the God and Goddess striking the objects with their magic power. Place the herbs and stones in the magic square or bag, tie, and set aside. Then take your tea bag, hold it in your hands, and say:

I charge this tea bag to bring prosperity, health, and happiness. With each sip of this tea I grow more prosperous. So mote it be.

Keep the tea to sip or drink on the following Sunday after

the September Equinox. Put another pinch of Prosperity Incense on the charcoal. As smoke rises thank the God and Goddess for coming into your sacred space and circle. Bid them farewell and release your circle, saying, *The circle is undone and not broken. I cast it into the universe for the good of all. So mote it be.*

Snuff out your candles or let them burn as long as you want. You may want to relight them at a time when you want to again cast the spell. Carry the spell and magic bag with you. Now you may wear your Mabon Oil on your wrist, back of the neck, and forehead for at least four more days. After the spell has been cast, you may use the charged incense as often as you wish.

HOLIDAY FARE

Mabon is a Witch's Thanksgiving, a time to appreciate and give thanks to the Goddess for her bounty and to share in the joys of the harvest. Mabon is ruled by the Wine Moon and marks the completion of the fruit harvest. Peaches, apples, grapes, gourds, and pumpkins are plentiful. The grains of Summer are now dry and ready to be stored, and what fruits and vegetables we do not eat now we preserve and pickle for later use during Winter.

For a Witch, the holiday feast is sumptuous, not only for body but for soul. I think we all would agree that food is sacred, but few of us prepare and eat meals with the purpose of honoring the Earth. When we prepare food, especially for a holiday celebration, we do not simply stir, blend, or beat a set list of ingredients from a neatly clipped recipe. Witches try to bring ingredients into balance—a gentle touch of herbs here, a generous round of honey nectar there—whatever it takes to harmonize the energies of each with the energy of the whole, capturing both the goodness of taste and the magical essence of a meal.

A magically made meal, then, not only satisfies hunger but makes you feel good about yourself and reconnects you to the natural gifts of the Goddess. Drinking hot apple cider is an excellent example of a magical Mabon beverage that exacts a beneficial spiritual change. The apple rules the heart, and cider alone is a self-love potion. By spicing it with cinnamon, ruled by Jupiter and the Sun, it becomes an intoxicating drink of health, well-being, and prosperity. By drinking cider we are in essence ingesting the sunlight, and in a way mothering the Sun, just as Modron does for Mabon.

Following is a suggestion for a Mabon meal, but you can experiment with your own magical concoctions using foods and ingredients that are plentiful in your area.

FEAST OF MABON

Mabon Wine Moon Cider
Roast Chicken Rubbed with Sage, Basil, and Thyme
Acorn Squash Suffused with Sweet Butter, Cinnamon, and Honey
Candy Kelly's Magical Apple Bread

MABON WINE MOON CIDER

4 cups apple cider
4 cups grape juice
2 cinnamon sticks, 4 inches long
1 tsp. allspice
½ tsp. whole cloves
additional cinnamon sticks for cups, 6 inches long

In a 4-quart saucepan, heat cider and grape juice. Add cinnamon, allspice, and cloves. Bring just to boiling. Lower heat and simmer for 5 minutes. Serve with ladle from a cauldron. Makes 8 cups.

ROAST CHICKEN RUBBED WITH SAGE, BASIL, AND THYME

1 lemon
1 large whole roasting chicken
3 tbs. sweet butter, unsalted
3–4 sprigs fresh sage
3–4 sprigs fresh basil
3–4 sprigs fresh thyme

First squeeze the juice of the lemon into the chicken cavities. Dab pads of butter on the chicken. Rub lightly with 1 or 2 sprigs each of herbs. Roast chicken for approximately 1 hour at 350° F. Near end of roasting sprinkle on remainder of herbs, saving one or two for garnish.

ACORN SQUASH SUFFUSED WITH SWEET BUTTER, CINNAMON, AND HONEY

4 acorn squash
8 tbs. honey
8 tbs. sweet unsalted butter or margarine
8 tsp. cinnamon

Halve squash through midsections (not end to end). Remove seeds. Add 1 tablespoon each of honey and butter and 1 teaspoon each of cinnamon to squash halves. Loosely cover each half with aluminum foil and place on shallow baking sheet. Bake at 350° F for 1½ hours.

CANDY KELLY'S MAGICAL APPLE BREAD

3–4 shredded apples, with peels
2 eggs
¼ cup vegetable oil
¼ cup water
½ cup sugar or ¼ cup honey
½ tsp. each salt, cinnamon, baking powder, and baking soda
1 handful chopped walnuts (reserve some for topping)
½ handful raisins
2 cups flour
2 handfuls (palmfuls) oats

Mix apples and all ingredients except flour and oats. Beat well. Gently add flour and oats to mixture. Stir just until blended. Pour into greased and floured loaf pan. Sprinkle top with leftover walnuts, patting them down. Bake at 350° F for 1 hour.

ANCIENT ACTIVITIES

On holidays we often take part in many "traditional" activities without ever really knowing why we do so. Making wreaths, or using herbs in decorations around windows and doors, for example, have ancient significance beyond the fact that wreaths and swags look nice. A wreath creates the sacred shape of a circle. We decorate Autumn wreaths made of grape vine with bittersweet because bittersweet is for protection. By dressing up a wreath with ribbons of gold and yellow, sprigs of dried yarrow or cinnamon sticks, we bring in the warmth and energy of the Sun. The ancient tribes made wreaths around this time of year because it was cold outside and they wanted to bring warmth indoors.

Although we may not realize it as such, we make wreaths today for the same reason.

During the Mabon season materials are plentiful for making decorations and potpourris, Witch's cords, and children's toys. Following are a few suggestions for having some Mabon fun.

WITCH'S BROOM

Tie dried corn husks around a strong, relatively straight branch of your choice. Oak, maple, birch, or hickory work well. Using ribbon or string, decorate the broom with cat-o'-nine-tails or sprigs of bittersweet. Smaller brooms are ideal for hanging on a door or porch, while larger, more functional brooms can stand as an instrument of protection in a corner by an entrance. Witches usually leave their brooms near their doorways and always pointed up for protection. We believe that any negative energy that may darken a door will be neutralized by entering one end of the broomstick and traveling down, back up, and out.

MABON WREATH

Entwine a grape vine into a circle and fasten with either string or ribbon. If you can't find a grape vine, get a wire base from a florist. Attach sprigs of bittersweet and dried yarrow. Add ribbons, a Mabon Philtre (see p. 245), herbs, or any stone, jewelry, or charm ruled by the Sun and Jupiter.

MAGIC APPLE DOLLS

Apples are sacred symbols of the Witch. Our holy land, Avalon, means Apple-land or Island of Apples. Slice an apple through its midsection and its seeds reveal the sacred shape of the pentacle. You will need two large apples to make Mabon and Modron, two pencils or two dowels about twelve inches long, a paring knife, a glass or bowl of water to wash your fingers, a plate, and a towel to wipe your hands. Peel and core the apples. In order to carve a face in an apple, you need to understand a little bit about sculpturing. To make an eye, for example, don't cut a hole into the apple. Make wedges like indentations around the shape of the eye, so the eye is raised from the apple's surface. The same applies for making a nose. Cut wedges around it. You want the apple's features to protrude. Do the same with the mouth, leaving the lips mounded. If you want it to pout, make a line across the mound. If you want to get fancy, cut wedges around cheekbones or ears to make them more pronounced.

Place apples on a dowel and put them into a jar where they can stand up to dry. Prepare these long before Mabon and charge in Magic Circles. After two to three weeks they shrink, looking like shrunken faces and heads. You can embellish these if you wish. Some paint them gold or leave them natural and then turn them into dolls. Use wheat, doll's hair, or dried herbs for hair. Some make tiny robes and capes and bring them into the Magic Circle, asking the Goddess and God to charge them with their light.

You can also hang the Mabon and Modron heads on a Witch's cord or Mabon wreath. To hang them on a cord, you need three strands of cord in Mabon colors about three yards long. Holding three strands of cord in your hands, tie three knots, then string an apple head. Tie three more knots, and thread another. Tie three more knots and you have a magical ninefold knotwork cord that you can hang over a doorway or entryway.

Faery Magic

Unless you have Faery blood inside you, it can be difficult to see the Faeries by looking directly at them. Often we are only able to catch glimpses of them in our peripheral field of vision. As we saw in the last chapter, however, a cat's eyes can act as a doorway to the Faery world. Pools, lakes, water in a cauldron, starlight, and crystals are other examples of thresholds to the Faery world.

Autumn is a gorgeous season to get outside and in touch with your natural surroundings. The following game is a simple way to have some fortune-telling fun while enjoying the best that the Mabon landscape has to offer. While the objects you are asked to look for seem ordinary enough, they are in fact Faery runes that can be used in Faery divination. A lost key, feathers, an interesting bottle with no flat bottom—these are strange and beautiful things that you tend to find serendipitously. Actually, you don't really find them at all. They come to you! The Faery Queen Oonach can help you with divinations or quests any time of the year. She is radiant with stars and has golden hair. To call her, you can use a Faery bell, or any round silver bell. For the following game, especially if it's your first time out, you should definitely ask the Faeries for some help.

Mabon Quest

Somewhere, but preferably in the great outdoors, find a white feather (for purity or to send harm away), a black feather (for material things to come, like surprises), and a blue feather (for messages of happiness). Gather three acorns, marking each with a Magic Marker (red for love, green for money, and black for health). Find a twig from an oak tree (for male) and tie an orange string to it so you know it's from an oak tree; then find a twig from an apple tree (for love) and tie a red string to it. Find a white stone (for things to be sent outward), a black stone (for things to come to you), and a gray stone (for things that may or may not happen). If playing the game with Witches, charge all the items in a Magic Circle. If not, then place items in a sacred space, perhaps during the Mabon meal. Write down on paper what each item stands for. Place all the items in a box and shake. Each person playing then asks a question he or she wants an answer to. Without looking, reach in and pick an item. If the answer seems ambiguous, pick again. For example, picking out the apple twig and a black stone means "love is coming," a green acorn and black stone means "money is coming," and so on.

Penny's Star Trip

The September evenings of Mabon are clear and crisp, but not so cool that you can't go outside at night. It is the perfect time to enjoy the stars. Of course, on Mabon we try to focus on the Sun. We try to draw it in, remember it, and respect it. But even in the dark, there is the light of the Sun, for what are stars but remembrances of the Sun, long-ago reflections of light.

One evening in September, my daughter Penny discovered a wonderful way to get connected to the magic of the Earth and stars.

Perhaps the hardest part about taking this "trip" is finding a spot where you can actually lie down and see the stars. If you live in an urban area, this can be tough to find. In any case, if you are able to, get a blanket, lie down, and stare at the stars for half an hour. Do not look at your peripheral field of vision. Look at the sky only. Study the stars. Bring a timer with you so you know when a half hour is up—you don't want to have to raise your arm to keep looking at your watch. At the end of half an hour, lift your arms toward the sky, reaching out for your star. You'll feel as though you're falling off the Earth—as though you're falling into the sky. You have in fact "lost touch" with the Earth, but you've gotten in touch with space and the reality of the stars. If you want to stop the ride, simply put your hand on the ground, or if you want to be really dramatic, roll over onto your stomach and kiss the Earth.

APPENDIX

★

SOME BASIC ELEMENTS OF WITCHCRAFT

Following are a few brief descriptions of some basic elements used in practicing Witchcraft. For a more in-depth analysis of each, you may refer to my previous book on the Craft, *Power of the Witch: The Earth, the Moon, and the Magical Path to Enlightenment* (Dell Publishing, 1989).

Pentacles

A pentacle is a five-pointed star in a circle. It is a sacred symbol of the Witch and has a long, rich history. The star is always drawn in one continuous stroke, and we always wear the pentacle with its top point facing upward. The pentacle represents the five senses of humankind through which we gain knowledge about the Earth and ourselves. The circle surrounding the star is the Magic Circle of life, the God/Goddess, the Wheel of the Year, and the encircling power of the All. It represents universal wisdom.

Peyton

A peyton is a large pentacle often used in ritual to point out the four directions and to draw in all energies. It is usually cut out of brass or silver and is about four to six inches in diameter.

The Four Directions

These are, of course, North, South, East, and West. Depending on where the altar faces, we walk deosil, or clockwise, stopping at each point to call on the four directions, and widdershins, or counterclockwise, to bid them farewell.

The Four Elements

These are, of course, Earth, Air, Fire, and Water, which coincide with the four directions. When we cast a Magic Circle, we call on the four elements to bring a balance of these collective energies in Nature to the sacred space.

Casting the Magic Circle

Casting a Magic Circle creates a magic space as well as time for you to perform magic. The traditional circle is nine feet in diameter. If you live in cramped quarters, you can still cast a Magic Circle. Nine feet is simply the magical ideal. To cast, the High Priestess walks three times clockwise around the circle, pointing with her wand well extended beyond her body. She says: *I cast this circle to protect us from all negative and positive forces and energies that may come to do us harm. I charge this circle to draw in only the most perfect, powerful, correct, and harmonious forces and energies that will be compatible with our magic. I cast this circle to serve as a sacred space between the world, a place of love and perfect trust. So mote it be.* Once the circle is cast, it cannot be broken. Don't even have a telephone cord crossing the perimeter and make sure you don't have any animals roaming about. No one must leave the circle until it is opened at the end of the ritual by the High Priestess. To open the circle, walk three times counterclockwise and say, *The circle is open, but never undone.*

Alpha

Alpha is the scientific base of all Witchcraft and magic. It is an altered state of consciousness associated with relaxation, meditation, and dreaming. In alpha, the mind is receptive to different avenues of communication like telepathy, clairvoyance, and precognition. Going into alpha takes practice. Indeed, an entire book could be written just on alpha. I teach an easy method for going into alpha using colors and numbers. I call this the Crystal Countdown. To put yourself in alpha, find a quiet space, close your eyes, and relax, breathing deeply. When you feel balanced and relaxed, visualize an empty screen in your mind's eye. Next, see on the screen a red 7. Hold it on the screen, then release it. Next, bring up an orange 6. Hold it and release it. Count down the remaining spectrum of colors: yellow 5, green 4, blue 3, indigo 2, orchid 1. This sequence of colors appears in every rainbow and in every prismatic breakdown of light. When you get to orchid 1, count down from 10 to 1 to deepen the alpha state. Say to yourself: *I am now in alpha and everything I do will be accurate and correct, and this is so.* Now you can do whatever meditation or healing task you like. You can come out of alpha any time you wish. You are always in control in the alpha state and even partially aware of what's happening in the room. Bells do not sound off when you have reached alpha level. You can still hear and think. In fact you are reaching alpha as soon as you close your eyes. To count back up, erase what you have on the screen with your hands. Then give yourself a complete health clearance by placing your hand, palm downward, about six inches above your head. In one smooth motion bring your hand down in front of your face, chest, and stomach, while turning your palm outward and pushing away from you. Say: *I am healing myself and giving myself total health clearance.* This clears away any harmful or negative energies that may have been present while in alpha.

Instant Alpha Trigger

Witches use instant alpha when we are in places or situations where we can't relax or close our eyes, such as while driving a car. In order to be able to go into instant alpha, you must first go into a deep alpha state using the Crystal Countdown described above. While in alpha, cross the middle finger of your left hand over the top of your index finger. Say: *When I cross my fingers, I am in instant alpha.* Again, you may not "feel" as if you have gone into an altered state, but you have. Count yourself back up. Now you have triggered your mind's eye and programmed it with information that will allow you to go into alpha whenever you need to. Simply cross your fingers and you're there.

Basic Altar Setup

Many Witches face their altars East, but you can face your altar any way you wish as long as you understand the meaning behind the directions and the reason why you

chose what you chose. North faces mystery and constancy. East faces new life, rebirth, and beginnings. South faces motion and thought. West faces water, underwater worlds, and creation. You can place the representations of the four elements in any direction you wish, as well. I set my altar with Earth in the North, Fire in the East, Air in the South, and Water in the West. A stone or earth oil is a good representation for Earth. A candle represents Fire. Incense or an air plant is for Air, and a chalice of water or bowl of water for Water. A pentacle should focus the center of your altar. Your altar is a power spot with every object related to the magic you intend to do. You should have a black candle to draw in energy and a white candle to send energy out. Also, the Triple Goddess is often represented by white, red, and black candles. The altar doesn't have to be a fancy one. It could be an end table or even a kitchen table. The picture opposite shows many of the basic elements and placement of objects on the altar.

Charging Tools and Herbs

Charging tools and herbs is a way of transferring energy from you and the universe to an object. Your wand is the first tool that needs to be charged. Of course, you need a wand in order to cast a circle in which to charge your tools! You can still cast a circle using a four-and-a-half-foot cord and some sea salt from a gourmet food shop or Witch shop. Place your altar and all tools to be charged in the center. Place one end of the cord in the center. At the open end start walking off your circle clockwise from the North, sprinkling sea salt to make the circle's mark. One foot in, mark off another circle with your sea salt. And one foot in from there, mark off a third. Your circle is cast. To charge tools, go into alpha, pass your hands over the wand in a sweeping motion, and say: *I neutralize any incorrect energy in this wand.* Then hold the wand with both hands and say: *I charge this wand to catalyze my every thought and deed by my will. I ask that this be correct and for the good of all. So mote it be.* Now you can use your wand to cast circles and to charge other magical objects.

MOONS AND CORRESPONDENCES

January: Wolf Moon. Protection, confidence, strength.

February: Chaste Moon. Maiden Goddess Brid, fertility, strength.

March: Seed Moon. Seeds of plants, fruits, vegetables, seed of success, spirituality.

April: Hare Moon. Goddess Ostera, fertility, growth, wisdom.

May: Faery Moon. Faery power, wisdom, love, romance, good health.

June: Mead Moon. Marriage, love, romance, abundance, career, success, health.

July: Herb Moon. Strength, magical potency, herb harvest, health, success.

August: Barley Moon. Grain Goddesses and Sun Gods, grain harvest, bounty, agriculture, fertility, marriage, good health.

September: Wine Moon. Grape and fruit harvest, life's blood, protection, confidence, strength.

October: Blood Moon. Meat harvest, remembrance, protection, stability, New Year's resolutions.

November: Snow Moon. Frost Faeries, hope, protection, warmth, healing.

December: Oak Moon. Merlin, Oak King, goodwill, peace, protection, love.

SACRED TREES OF THE CELTS

Rowan: Powerful wood of the *sidhe,* great for wands and cauldron fires, used for magical divination and protection. Its berries feed the Faeries.

Alder: Bran's tree. Death-in-life aspect because it doesn't die in Winter. Good for sovereignty wand and for strength. Its flowers make green dye, and its bark red dye.

Willow: Wands are used for weddings and Witch brooms. Good for beauty and love.

Ash: Protector. Never cut down by the Celts. Its wood is used in many staffs for psychic strength, power, and healing.

Hawthorn: Only brought into the house at Beltane. It harbors the Faeries and should never be destroyed. Good for music, poetry, and psychic ability.

Oak: Mighty and sacred. Oak groves are great places to do magic. Oak struck by lightning is most powerful. Acorn is for invisibility, all magical powers, strength, and fertility. Merlin's favorite tree.

Holly: Sun King. Used for fertility, protection, is steadfast in adversity, increases strength, and helps you to win against hardships and challenges.

Hazel: Helps you to become a person of many arts and skills. Heightens the five senses.

Apple: Sacred tree of Avalon or Apple Land or Island of Apples. Three apples are hung on the sacred silver branch wand. Good for healing the sick, helping you to sleep, protecting your heart. An apple cut through the middle forms the Witch's star, a pentacle in middle.

Grapevine: Underworld and Merrow associations. Power of the Triple Goddess, the Morrighan. Giver of life.

Ivy: The feminine side of holly, but very strong. Symbol of endurance, stability, and deep psychic powers. Ruled by Saturn.

Water reed or broom plant: Its flexible twigs bend and connect this world with the underwater realms.

Blackthorn: Weapon of protection, neutralizes anything bad that can happen.

Elder: Symbol of the "Good God," the Dagda. Good for many skills and arts and stability. Its berries are used for rouge and coloring skin.

Fir: A sacred tree of life and death. Merlin and Vivian's tree. Symbol of sovereignty and gift of knowledge.

Furze (gorse): Good for protection because its stalk has thorny spikes. Its golden blossoms are symbols of the Sun. Also is used for chastity and faithfulness.

Heather: For wealth, protection, knowledge, open-mindedness, luck, and flower crowns.

Aspen: Good for relieving pain, strong against weather or wind, helps you to pass on to Avalon.

Yew: Life-in-death and death-in-life aspects of the Goddess. The eternal cycle of life.

SOURCES

American Mead Association
P.O. Box 206
Ostrander, OH 43061

Aphrodisia (an herb shop)
62 Kent Street
Brooklyn, NY 11222
1-800-221-6989
(mail order and store)

Bunratty Mead (imported from Claire, Ireland)
Camelot Importing Co., Inc.
P.O. Box 146
Old Bridge, NJ 08857
201-670-1866

Crow Haven Corner (a Witch shop)
125 Essex Street
Salem, MA 01970
508-745-8763
(Laurie Cabot products available, mail order and store)

Magic Door
(Laurie Cabot products, potions, and magic tools)
P.O. Box 8349
Salem, MA 01971-8349
508-744-6274
(Wholesale only)

Temple of Nine Wells
P.O. Box 281
Salem, MA 01970
508-740-0334

White Light Pentacles/Sacred Spirit Products
P.O. Box 8163
Salem, MA 01970
508-745-8668
(Wholesale only)

FURTHER READING

Books

Bain, Iain. *Celtic Knotwork.* New York: Sterling Publishing Co., Inc., 1992.

Cabot, Laurie with Cowan, T. *Power of the Witch: The Earth, the Moon, and the Magical Path to Enlightenment.* New York: Dell Publishing, 1989.

———. *Love Magic: The Way to Love Through Rituals, Spells, and the Magical Life.* New York: Dell Publishing, 1992.

Conway, D. J. *Celtic Magic.* St. Paul, MN: Llewellyn Publications, 1990.

Cross, T. P., and Slover, C. H. *Ancient Irish Tales.* Dublin: Figgis, 1936.

Cunningham, Scott. *The Magic in Food.* St. Paul, Minn.: Llewellyn Publishing, 1990.

Evans-Wentz, W. Y. *The Fairy Faith in Celtic Countries.* Library of the Mystic Arts. New York: Citadel Press/Carol Publishing Group, 1990.

Fell, Barry. *America B.C.: Ancient Settlers in the New World.* New York: Pocket Books, 1976.

Frazier, Sir James George. *The Golden Bough.* New York: The Macmillan Company, 1951.

The Mabinogion. Translated and introduced by Jeffrey Gantz. New York: Dorset Press, 1985.

Macbain, Alexander. *Celtic Mythology and Religion.* Stirling Eneas Mackay, 1917.

Matthews, Caitlin. *Mabon and the Mysteries of Britain: An Exploration of the Mabinogion.* London: Arkana/The Penguin Group, 1987.

Matthews, John. *The Song of Taliesin: Stories and Poems from the Books of Broceliande.* London: The Aquarian Press/HarperCollins, 1991.

Merne, John G. *A Handbook of Celtic Ornament.* Dublin: Mercier Press, 1990.

Rutherford, Ward. *The Druids: Magicians of the West.* Wellingborough, England: The Aquarian Press, 1983.

Spence, Lewis. *The Magic Arts in Celtic Britain.* New York: Samuel Weiser, Inc./The Rider Company, 1970.

———. *The Minor Traditions of British Mythology.* New York: The Arno Press, 1979.

Journals

The Green Egg
P.O. Box 1542
Ukiah, CA 95482

Fire Heart
Box 462
Maynard, MA 01754

The Herb Companion
Interweave Press, Inc.
201 East 4th Street
Loveland, CO 80537

Magical Blend Magazine
P.O. Box 600
Chico, CA 95927-0600